# HORRIBLY

# TUTANKHAMUN

## AND HIS TOMBFUL OF TREASURE

by Michael Cox

*Illustrated by Clive Goddard*

**■ SCHOLASTIC**

Scholastic Children's Books,
Euston House, 24 Eversholt Street,
London NW1 1DB, UK

A division of Scholastic Ltd
London ~ New York ~ Toronto ~ Sydney ~ Auckland
Mexico City ~ New Delhi ~ Hong Kong

Published in the UK by Scholastic Ltd, 2007

10 digit ISBN 1 407 10519 1
13 digit ISBN 978 1407105 19 2

All rights reserved
Printed in the UK by CPI Bookmarque, Croydon, CR0 4TD

4 6 8 10 9 7 5

# CONTENTS

## INTRODUCTION

NAME A FAMOUS EGYPTIAN PHARAOH!

KING TUTANKHAMUN!

During ancient Egypt's astonishing 3,000 years of world supremacy it was ruled by hundreds of different Pharaohs. But out of all those mega-powerful kings, the one most of us can name is King Tutankhamun. Not because we have access to amazingly detailed and fascinating records of his life and achievements. Nor because we know for certain that he led conquering armies which terrified Egypt's neighbours into handing over riches and slaves. Nor because he had enormous pyramids and temple-like burial chambers built to house his own remains and those of his family. No, it's none of those things.

It's simply because a go-getting British archaeologist called Howard Carter had a dream that he would one day discover that rarest of all archaeological finds: a Pharaoh's tomb, complete with its mummy and treasures, left more or less untouched for thousands of years.

And, after enduring year after year of depressing disappointments, during which he found nothing but rock and sand...

AND YET MORE ROCK!

...Howard eventually struck gold! Both figuratively *and* literally! Because he discovered that undreamed-of cache of riches: Tutankhamun and his tombful of treasures.

And ever since the amazing day when Howard entered the 'lost Pharaoh's' tomb, millions of people the world over have gazed upon Tutankhamun and his treasures and been utterly awestruck by what they have seen.

However, in many cases, knowing that Tut was a Pharaoh who met an early death, is about as far as their own treasure-trove of knowledge goes. But there's a lot more to the amazing tale of King Tut and his treasures than that! For instance, did you know that...

• He became the leader of the world's number-one superpower and its fearsome armies at an age when most other boys were still playing with their *toy* soldiers. In other words, when he was just nine years old!

• Tutankhamun married his 15-year-old sister – also when he was just nine!

• He met a very, *very* sticky end – possibly in more ways than one!

• His remains were said to be guarded by a huge cobra. And on the very day that Howard Carter entered Tut's tomb, the archaeologist's own pet canary was killed ... by a huge cobra!

• Amateur archaeologist Theodore Davies found the crucial clues to the whereabouts of Tut's lost tomb 15 years before it was discovered. But *he* thought they were nothing more than 'a load of old rubbish', so he gave them away!

If you want to uncover more about these amazing tales, not to mention oodles of facts and stories about the perfidious plots of power-mad potentates, the ancient Egyptian art of drip-drying dead bodies, the catastrophic consequences of calamitous curses, and much, much more ... simply grab your archaeologist's pick and shovel, then dig deep – into the astonishing story *Tutankhamun and his Tombful of Treasure*!

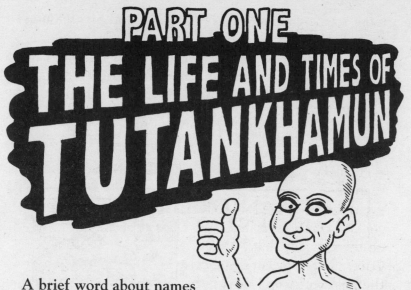

# PART ONE
# THE LIFE AND TIMES OF TUTANKHAMUN

## A brief word about names

Egyptian rulers had lots of names and, to make matters worse, some of them seemed to change them more often than they changed their underwear. King Tutankhamun, for example, was first called Tutankhaten, but changed his name to Tutankhamun two years after he became king. And his dad, Akhenaten, was originally Amenhotep IV. However, for the sake of clarity, sanity, personal hygiene and continuity, throughout the course of *this* book, Tutankhamun will be referred to as Tutankhamun, Tut, (or Old Pointy-Head), while his dad will be referred to as Akhenaten.

## An even briefer word about dates

No one knows for sure exactly when Tutankhamun was born or when he died. So all the dates used in Part One of this book are very approximate. But one thing we do know is that his story took place an awfully long time ago!

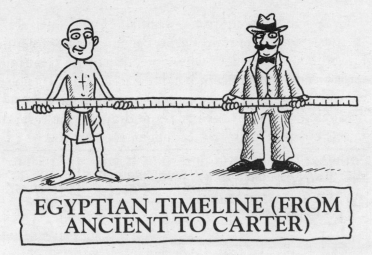

# EGYPTIAN TIMELINE (FROM ANCIENT TO CARTER)

**7000 BC** Wandering tribes of people begin to arrive in the Nile Valley and think…

They create scattered settlements that eventually grow to become the Upper and Lower Egyptian Kingdoms.

**3000 BC** The Kingdoms finally agree a merger deal. Things really come on apace now. The dynastic era begins, i.e. successive royal families rule the country for long periods. Business booms, trade flourishes and (most) people prosper.

Once stability, security and wealth are established, not-in-the-least-bit-ancient Egypt becomes a confident, forward-looking society where breathtakingly beautiful art is created, magnificent buildings are erected, cutting-edge technology is developed, great mathematical and medicinal advances take place and an elaborate and hugely complex 'pick 'n' mix' religious system flourishes!

The Egyptians even invented a new-fangled writing system with its very own alphabet.

And they were the first people to decide that there were 365 days in a year!

And so, with the exception of the occasional famine, foreign invasion and local revolution, it all carries on for another fun-filled 2,500 years. But then, around the time that the 25th royal dynasty is in power, things begin to look a bit shaky.

**700 BC** Assyrians from Mesopotamia (now known as Iraq) conquer and rule Egypt.

**525 BC** Persians (or Iranians as they're now known) conquer Egypt.

**332 BC** Shy and unassuming Greek warrior and collector-of-other-people's countries, Alexander the Great, conquers Egypt.

**31 BC** The Romans conquer and rule Egypt.

**AD 642** The Arabs conquer and rule Egypt.

**1250–1517** The Mamelukes (freed Turkish slaves) conquer and rule Egypt.

11

**1517** The Turks rule Egypt.

**1798** Napoleon Bonaparte
invades and takes over
Egypt.

**1801** Helped by British, the Turks chuck out Napoleon
and Egypt once more becomes part of the Turkish
Empire.

**1882** British troops take
over Egypt and it becomes
part of the British Empire.

**1922** Amazingly kind,
generous and caring Great
Britain gives Egypt its
independence. King Fu'ad I
takes over.

**So, what else was happening in 1922?**
• The Austin Seven made the new-fangled 'motoring'
craze popular in Britain
• The USSR (Union of Soviet Socialist Republics) was
created
• King George V opened the brand-new concrete tennis
stadium at Wimbledon
• The British imprisoned Mahatma Gandhi (soon-to-be
leader of India)
• The BBC began the first-ever radio service in the
United Kingdom

• Ralph Samuelson became the first person to ski on water
  Oh yes, there was one more thing...
  A British archaeologist called Howard Carter dug a
hole in the desert and found something rather
remarkable, stunning, exciting and wonderful!

# The Morning Times

### 23 November 1922  Britain's Leading Daily

# SENSATIONAL! AMAZING! STUNNING!

**Tutankhamun's tombful of treasure finally found by Howard Carter**

'Awesome!'
Anne Egyptologist
'Incredible!'
Archie Ologist
(...and that was just the bloke
feeding the donkeys!)

Dynamic Digger
Discovers Dazzling
Treasure Trove In Desert

# ALL SORTS OF GODS FOR ALL SORTS OF BODS

To really get the most out of the astounding tale of *Tutankhamun and his Tombful of Treasure*, you've got to know something about the world the Egyptians inhabited and their ideas about it. Quite simply, they believed that the world was flat, and consisted of a sort of huge pizza base, made from mud, rock and sand, floating in the middle of an enormous sea, which fed the river Nile.

Important note for readers with a tenuous grasp of geography: we now know this not to be the case. Egypt is, in fact, a hot and dry country situated at the northern end of the African continent.

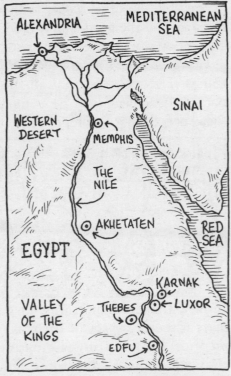

Most of it is infertile desert. But the flood plain of the river Nile is very, very fertile indeed, because of the 'inundation' that takes place each year. These floods are caused by all the water that has gathered during the rainy season in the mountains and hills of countries like Ethiopia and Uganda, suddenly rushing down the Nile and filling the valley with black mud. This was very handy indeed because **a)** it hardly ever rains in Egypt, **b)** the mud was so fertile you could throw a shirt button in it and, encouraged by the brilliant Egyptian sun, it would instantly grow into something good to eat (well, almost), and **c)** mixed with straw and dried in the sun, the mud made excellent building bricks.

Coupled with the fact that the Nile was full of good things to eat *and* also provided the Egyptians with a ready-made 'wetter-way' on which they could travel from north to south and back again in their skiffs, barges and yachts, they more or less had it made. In fact, the ancient Greek tourist and brainbox Herodotus described Egypt as the 'gift of the Nile'. In other words, without the big, wet wiggly thing and all the good stuff it brought, the great Egyptian civilization would never have existed.

However, the Egyptians had a slightly different take on things. *They* believed that all these useful and reliable natural phenomena were there simply because the enormous squad of gods they worshipped had organized it that way!

In fact, the Egyptians' army of gods played important parts in every aspect of their day-to-day lives. Not to mention being a truly fascinating bunch of colourful characters whose adventures, family shenanigans and shape-shifting capers would rival the likes of Spiderman, Shrek and the Simpsons.

## All sorts of gods for all sorts of bods

Nowadays, all sorts of people all over the world worship all sorts of gods. It was much the same in ancient Egypt, but in fact, the Egyptians had over 2,000 different gods to choose from! Kings had their individual 'life-coach' gods who gave them tips on how to rule, how not to look a fool, how to look cool, and so on. Workers, priests, merchants and peasants had their own 'personal-trainer' gods who were all incredibly knowledgeable and helpful when it came to handing out tips and advice about their different jobs and professions. The gods really were an approachable and user-friendly bunch, who behaved in much the same way as their mortal worshippers down on Earth, drinking, thinking, laughing, crying and dying.

The gods moved up and down a god-popularity league table according to whichever king happened to be in power and what sort of mood they were in at the time. For instance, the maker of all things was either Re, Amun, Ptah, Khnum or Aten, depending on which version of the Egyptian creation myth was currently fashionable. Just so you know who was top of the gods' league table, here's a quick-fact-fix temple's-worth of Egypt's most high-profile deities. And who better to start with than big Re himself!

# The God Squad

## Re

**Appearances:** A falcon-headed man wearing a sun-disc on his head, or a dung beetle. NB: the dung beetle wasn't on his head – he *was* the dung beetle! The actual shape of the sun (the disc) was represented by another god called Aten. Remember him – he figures significantly in Tutankhamun's story!

**Jobs:** Re or Amun Re, as he was also known, was the sun god and the supreme judge of the dead, and for this reason he was regarded by most Egyptians as the ultimate all-singing, all-dancing mega-god!

**God gossip:** Re travelled through the waters of heaven in two different boats. His first boat, Madjet, rose out of the east. The second boat, a small barge called Semektet, took Re to sunset in the west. The gods Horus and Maat navigated the boats for Re.

Re's night-time route was always blocked by three monsters that he had to fight and defeat every single night if the sun was going to come up the next day. Apep, the darkness monster, was the most powerful of the three. If he ever defeated Re, the weather the next day was stormy. Stormy weather is rare in Egypt so it was generally thought that Re did a good job (and still does for that matter!).

HOORAY FOR RE!

### Maat

**Appearance:** Maat was a woman wearing the feather of truth in her hair (its name was also Maat). Sometimes she kneeled with her arms outstretched like wings.

**Jobs:** If you were a *good* Egyptian, you would have spent a lot of time thinking about Maat. Because, not only was she a goddess, but she was also a way of life. This goddess stood for goodness, harmony, justice, truth and order. In short, she was everything that Seth (see below) was not!

**God gossip:** Rulers like King Tutankhamun were supposed to run their kingdoms according to the principles of Maat, making sure that every single person was treated with kindness, fairness, honesty and respect.

### Osiris

**Appearance:** Mummy with green skin, wearing a white crown.

**God gossip:** Ex-king of Egypt, Osiris was murdered by his brother, Seth, who then chopped his body to bits. However, his sister, Isis, put him back together again and bandaged him up. Then, after becoming the first-ever Egyptian to have been mummified, he went on to become king of the Afterworld. And, most importantly of all, when Tutankhamun was crowned king of all Egypt, *he* became the living embodiment of Osiris here on Earth, as did all Egyptian Pharaohs.

JUST LOOK AT HIM. HE THINKS HE'S GOD'S GIFT TO EGYPTIANS!

## Seth

**Appearances:** A pig-like animal, a pig, a black hippo, a dog with an arrow-like tail, a crocodile, or a man with red hair and eyes, wearing a red robe.

**Jobs:** God of storms, evil, deserts, confusion and all-round stroppiness.

**God gossip:** Seth was the permanent enemy of Horus, the son of Osiris. He was one of Egypt's oldest gods and the Egyptians feared him because he was so dangerous, yet they also admired his strength and ferocity.

## Thoth

**Appearance:** Ibis-headed man. Both the ibis and the ape were sacred to him.

**Jobs:** Inventor of writing. Scribbling notes for other gods. Recording the decisions made about the dead who were tried in the Hall of Judgement, inscribing the sacred persea tree with the number of years a king had allotted to him for his reign (which, in King Tut's case, wasn't all that many!).

**God gossip:** Thoth was believed to have a book containing all the wisdom of the world.

WOULD YOU LIKE TO PHONE A FRIEND?

YES PLEASE, I'D LIKE TO PHONE THOTH!

## Anubis

**Appearance:** Man with jackal's head.

**Jobs:** Guiding the dead on the paths through the Underworld. Helping mummify the body of Osiris, the god who was killed by Seth. Listening to prayers for the dead. Being the patron-god of mummifiers and overseeing the embalming process. All in all, a very busy god.

**God gossip:** At one time, Anubis was the great god of funerals and the lord and guardian of the necropolis (burial place) but he was eventually downgraded in favour of Osiris. Several really terrifying statues of Anubis stood guard in King Tut's tomb. Egyptians often saw jackals scavenging in their cemeteries and therefore associated them with watching over the dead.

21

## MEET THE FAMILY!

### Pharaohs a-go-go

Tut was a member of the line of Egyptian kings and queens known as the 18th dynasty, which ruled during what was called the New Kingdom period – generally a time of great prosperity and confidence, with lots of strong-minded and successful rulers. He was born some time around 1343 BC, but no one's entirely, 100 per cent sure who his parents were! Egyptian kings often married their sisters, and sometimes even their own *daughters* and *granddaughters*, so their family trees were often more like monkey puzzles than spreading oaks!

TUT'S FAMILY TREE

Thutmose → Kiya
↓ ↘ Amrose
POSSIBLY ← Hatshepsut OR
? ? ? → Smenkare
Nefertiti ←
Tut ?

As a result, historians, university professors, archaeologists and Egyptologists the world over, have collectively spent several centuries arguing about who was who in Tut's family. And they're still at it!

TUTANKHAMUN'S PARENTS WERE SMENKARE AND NEFERTITI

HOW **COULD** THEY BE? SMENKARE **WAS** NEFERTITI!

NO HE WASN'T! HE WAS TUTANKHAMUN'S BROTHER!

WELL I THINK HIS MUM AND DAD WERE AMENHOTEP IV AND KIYA!

RUBBISH! THEY WERE NEFERTITI... AND THAT GREAT BIG BLOKE OUT OF GLADIATOR!

YOU SEE THAT DUNG BEETLE, THAT'S YOUR SISTER, THAT IS!

Of course, not all this speculation about Tut's rellies was simply flights of fantasy and wild theorizing. All manner of painstaking archaeological and scientific research has been carried out in the search for the truth about his family. But even that occasionally throws up confusing or unreliable evidence.

**An Egyptogist reports...**
Just so you appreciate what a headache it is unravelling Tutankhamun's tangled family tree, here's a brief round-up of some of the facts and investigation results that have led to us sticky-beak Egyptologists knowing so much (and so little) about the golden boy's various rellies.

**a)** An inscription from a monument that had originally stood in Akhetaten, the holy city built by his dad, calls Tutankhamun a 'king's son'.

**b)** Pictures on King Akhenaten's tomb wall show a royal fan-bearer standing next to Queen Kiya's bed fanning a woman holding a baby. That baby is generally presumed to be the king-to-be!

**c)** One of the ways in which we learned boffins have tried to discover who was related to who in Tut's mysterious family background is to compare the skulls of various mummies to see if they have anything in common, which might suggest they are closely related.

After studying the skulls of Tutankhamun and Smenkhkare, some experts decided that their bone-domes were so similar they were probably brothers. However, other experts said, 'Hang on a mo'! If their bonces are so similar, it could also mean that Tutankhamun was King Smenkhkare's son! Or possibly even his dad!'

**d)** Other Egyptologists have suggested that Tutankhamun's dad and mum were really his grandad, Amenhotep III, and his grandma, the Great Royal Wife Tiye, because a lock of Tiye's hair was found in his tomb.

**e)** However, despite all the controversy surrounding the identity of Tut's folks, the most recent and widely accepted scholarly theory...

...about who was who, is that Tut's parents were King Akhenaten and Kiya, one of his wives. Queen Kiya's official title was 'Greatly Beloved Wife of Akhenaten' Among Akhenaten's other wives was Queen Nefertiti, world famous for her magnificent portrait sculpture, found by a German archaeologist in 1913. Akhenaten and Nefertiti had six daughters, whose names were,

Merytaten, Meketaten, Neferneferuaten-tasharit, Neferneferure, Sotepenre, Ankhesenpaaten (and the somewhat less well-known Knittingpaaten). These girls were therefore Tut's half-sisters, one of whom he would eventually marry, but not just yet, him only having just been born. And what a topsy-turvy world it was that he was born into!

## A right royal kerfuffle...

Tutankhamun was born in the middle of religious and political upheaval – all caused by his dad, Amenhotep IV. (Or Akhenaten, as he later renamed himself.)

For almost 2,000 years, things had remained more or less the same in the great civilization, with the Pharaohs enjoying their privileged and glamorous celebrity lifestyles, the scribes scribing, the armies conquering and the peasants happily farming the fertile mud of the Nile basin. And, most importantly, everyone thoroughly enjoyed their ever-popular polytheism, i.e. worshipping more gods than you could shake a high priest's tickling-stick at. But then – wouldn't you just know it – Akhenaten suddenly decided to go all weird and alternative, and turned Egypt on its head by saying that when it came to worship and religion everybody had completely had the wrong end of the stick for centuries. He declared that instead of there being hundreds of gods, there had only actually been one single god all along, namely Aten, who had previously been quite a minor and obscure sort of god (of course you remember him, he's the sun-disc god from page 17!). And when Akhenaten introduced his new one-god-fits-all 'monotheistic' religion to his entire kingdom it meant big changes, many of which were very, very unpopular:

**a)** All over the place all the other gods' regional offices and drop-in centres (i.e. their temples) were shut down.
**b)** With so many hundreds of gods suddenly not existing, the thousands of priests who'd formerly been their local earthly representatives were out of a job. Which, as you can imagine, made Akhenaten incredibly unpopular.

Tut's dad decided that his new 'monotheism' required a complete corporate-image makeover, including new logos, company colours, uniforms, etc. So, the Egyptian art that was associated with religion – i.e. *all* art! – changed radically in its appearance and meaning. Among these changes, art became far more laid back, personal and chilled-out, with artists creating touching little stone carvings of everyday life, like this one showing Akhenaten and his wife Nefertiti holding hands.

Then, as part of his great rocking and rolling religious revolution, Akenhaten not only changed his name from Amenhotep IV to Akenhaten (which means 'one useful to Aten') but also decided that the old Egyptian capital city of Thebes and its hundreds of temples just wasn't good enough for the new single all-powerful god. So, not being a Pharaoh do things by halves, he had a great new godopolis called Akhetaten (the Horizon of Aten) built on the east bank of the River Nile, 500 kilometres (311 miles) north of the ex-capital Thebes. He moved his entire royal household there: wives, kids, army, servants, advisers, hangers-on, papyri library, kitchen sink, the lot! And of course, he took with him all the priests he hadn't sacked as part of his one-god 'clean sweep!'

And this was the place where little Tut popped into the world and spent the first nine years of his very short life.

But Akhenaten's new one-god hobby didn't stop there! He became so obsessed with his one-stop worship that he neglected his other kingly responsibilities.

GREAT PHARAOH, I NEED MORE SOLDIERS AND CHARIOTS. THE HITTITES* ARE REFUSING TO PAY THEIR TRIBUTES

DON'T BOTHER ME NOW! I'M BUSY WORSHIPPING THE ONE AND ONLY GOD

BLOOMING NEW-AGE WEIRDO!

By the time little Tut began toddling around the beautiful gardens and orchards of his dad's new palaces, chasing butterflies, eating worms and wearing not a stitch, there was an awful lot of muttering, plotting and political argy-bargy and manoeuvring going on – all of which would soon have a profound influence on the little chap's life (and possibly his death).

COO!

WHEE!

YIPPEE!

MUTTER MUTTER

MURMUR MURMUR

PRAY PRAY...

* The Hittites were enemies of the Egyptians who came from the region now known as Turkey.

Naturally, little Tut was blissfully ignorant of all this and concerned with far more important things, like being cuddled by Maia, his wet nurse*, learning to walk, playing with his toy crocodile and weeing in the royal fish pond. Time, though, marches on, and all good things must end. So before Tut could say...

...he was off to school and studying every known subject under the ancient Egyptian sun!

* Throughout history many royal persons have considered breast-feeding their babies beneath their dignity, so they get a woman servant called a wet nurse to do it for them.

# TUTANKHAMUN – *STUDENT OF EVERY SUBJECT UNDER THE SUN!*

### TUTANKHAMUN'S SECRET LOST PAPYRI DIARI

1336 BC Wow! It seems like only five drips of the water clock since I was enjoying my carefree life in the palace gardens, playing hide and seek with my big sisters, flying my toy bird and jumping in and out of the royal fish ponds.

But I have now been at my studies for two years! Along with the other boys from the palace, I go to lessons where we do things like chanting our number tables, learning the names of our great kings, drawing maps of our great empire and writing hieroglyphs on clay tablets called potsherds. Or if our teacher, Old Crocodile chops, is in a really good mood, on papyrus, which is very, very expensive!

Crocodile chops is a wrinkled old reptile who makes us work like Nubian* slaves. And us the children of the highest nobles in the land. Hmmph! As we sit cross-legged with our writing tablets on our laps, he stands over us like a gang-master at the royal building works, tapping the palm of his hand with his wicked hippo-hide strap, his lizard eyes flicking this way and that, desperate to spot one of us slacking so that he can beat us. One boy in my group, Maazba, the son of a top army general, got a right thrashing from Crocodile chops, just because he didn't finish writing out his hieroglyphs on time. Mamba says he's going to get his dad to have him sent to fight the Hittites.

Or fed to the cheetahs in the Royal Zoo. Good!

I am really looking forward to seeing Crocodile chops eaten alive.

* The Nubians were subjects of the ancient Egyptians who lived in the area now known as Sudan.

In addition to learning his number tables, his country's history and geography and how to write hieroglyphs, another thing Tut would have been taught about at school was his body. The Egyptians had very definite and clear-cut ideas about which bit went where and what did what. However, rather like their grasp of big-picture geography, their knowledge and beliefs about the function and importance of various body organs was somewhat confused. Especially their beliefs about that incredibly important organ, the heart.

## The heart of the matter

Dr Jackal writes...

My Dear Young Tutankhamun
Re your enquiry about your heart and your afterlife.
Look after your heart! Without it... you're nothing! For starters, if you didn't have your heart you wouldn't be able to think! And if you didn't have your heart you wouldn't be able to remember stuff! And, most importantly of all if you didn't have your heart you'd have nowhere to keep your soul!
So it stands to reason that your heart is in charge of every single bit of the rest of your body. If it thinks, 'Feet shuffle in the sand!',

your feet shuffle in the sand.
And if it thinks, 'Hands make a ridiculous movement!', they make it!
And what's more, it sends your tears, spit, snot, food, poo and wee, all whooshing around your body! Which is why it's got all those tubes coming out of it!
Heartiest best wishes,
Dr Jackal

P.S. Re your enquiry as to why we have a brain. Forget it! That great blob of pink and grey jelly that sits in your skull is a complete waste of space. The only thing it does, is make snot!

## TUTANKHAMUN'S SECRET LOST PAPYRI DIARI

1336 BC Today we have been reading round the class (all six of us) from our papyrus scrolls. Talk about tedious. I tell you, I was bored out of my heart and kept daydreaming about going hunting for wild ducks with my brilliant new pet puppy. But Crocodile chops says

QUACK!

BARK!

35

if we don't do our work we're all going to end up as irrigation-ditch diggers or laundry men on the banks of the Nile. And we all know what happens to clothes-washers!

CHOMP!

What piffle! We are all of royal blood and destined for lives of luxury, glory and privilege (well, I hope we are). Later, I asked Maazba why his dad hadn't had crocodile chops fed to the cheetahs and he said that when he suggested it, his dad gave him another beating for getting beaten in the first place! Then he made him write out, 'I must not abuse my privileged position' in hieroglyphs 100 times. Hieroglyphs can be such a pain at times! But I suppose they do come in useful. After school, I was visited by the royal barber who shaved all of my head, apart from my lock of youth, the hank of hair that hangs from one side of my royal skull. When I'm grown up I'll be having my head shaved completely and I'll wear a wig. Then I shall really miss my lock of youth!

# Picture this! Hieroglyphs

Egypt was the perfect place for the world's first-ever fully-fledged writing system to pop up. For a start there was all that sand to doodle in! And, even more importantly, for several months of each year, everyone was surrounded by acres and acres of squelchy Nile mud. It would only be a matter of time before some bright spark wrote something in the mud; possibly out of necessity.

And growing out of that Nile mud were all those acres and acres of papyrus reeds, which would be perfect for making the paper, pens and brushes with which the Egyptians would soon start scribbling down their history, wisdom, mathematical and scientific discoveries, ideas, mythology and shopping lists. So if the Egyptians hadn't invented a writing system they would have needed some very good excuses.

But they did! Consequently, for the first time ever, thoughts and experiences wouldn't die with their owners and it would be possible for all sorts of information to be conveyed to people in far-off places and future ages in a permanent recorded form. All without the originator of that information being present. For instance, information about the life and times of King Tutankhamun!

## How they did it

The really, really ancient Egyptians couldn't spell, which was entirely understandable, as they hadn't yet got round to inventing their alphabet. So, if they wished to either record something or communicate some information, they just drew simple little pictures, now known as pictographs, to indicate what they meant.

TRANSLATION: BEWARE OF THE CROCODILE

However, this was quite time-consuming, so eventually the pictures were simplified into symbols. And there was also the problem of expressing quite complicated and abstract ideas into picture writing. Not an easy thing to do! Try turning this sentence of the French author Marcel Proust into picture writing…

*Perhaps the immobility of the things that surround us is forced upon them by our conviction that they are themselves, and not anything else, and by the immobility of our conceptions of them.*

So, as the thriving society of the can-do, go-getting Egyptians became more and more complex and sophisticated, the new writing system was fine-tuned to meet the demands of a busy, ultra-modern, 3,000-year-old society. One way this happened was for the symbols to take on a dual function, much like the keys on a computer keyboard. They could either represent a) the actual object, a function that was indicated by a simple line under the pictograph, or b) a sound.

But what we really need is for someone with hands-on, real-time experience of that period in history to give us...

## Hieroglyphs made easy

Greetings from ancient Egypt (as it will be known by the time you read this)

Today I will teach you about reeding and writing.

Note to scribe: please read this bit to your charges very slowly as they might find it hard to grasp (especially if they aren't the sharpest pen in the writing box). And please, don't hesitate to chastise them if they aren't paying attention. OK here goes...

Here are 24 hieroglyphic symbols which each represent a single sound.

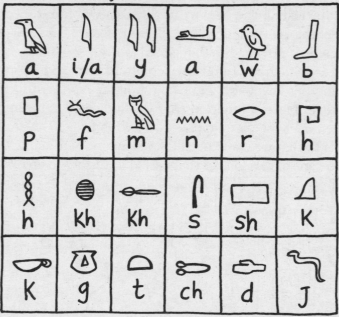

Pretty aren't they? 'Ah!' I hear you ask, 'Where are all the blinking vowels?' Well, we Egyptians don't really have vowels sounds in our written lingo. But does that mean we wander around talking like this?

cos that would be impossible wouldn't it?

GRRR! SHHH! HMM?

Of course we don't, you big hippopotamus's bottom! Use your dimwitted heart! We add the vowel sounds as we speak!

It takes a long time to learn to read hieroglyphs properly, especially as some of the signs represent more than one letter, or have some other meaning. Also, hieroglyphs can be read from left to right or from top to bottom. The trick is to see which way the pictured people and animals are facing, as that will always be the beginning of the sentence.

Yours superioroyally
Tut

## Cracked it!

When archaeologists first saw all those Egyptian hieroglyphs they were utterly bewildered by them. What was really frustrating was that there were millions of hieroglyphic scripts all over the place, carved and painted on tomb walls, chunks of stone and coffins, and written on papyrus.

The archaeologists knew that before them lay oodles of information. But it was all locked up in the tantalizing and inscrutable secret code known as hieroglyphs.

Then, in 1799, the historians and code-crackers got their phenomenally lucky break. While they were busy digging foundations for a new fort at Rosetta on the Nile delta, some of Napoleon's soldiers unearthed a slab of black basalt stone. On it was written an inscription dating from the year 196 BC. This doesn't sound like much to hieroglyph home about, until you realize that next to the extensive Egyptian hieroglyphic text on the

stone was a Greek translation of the very *same* text that *could* be read and understood by scholars of ancient Greek! So the ever-inquisitive Egyptologists now had the key to unlocking all those hieroglyphic secrets!

During the following decades, masses of information was discovered from the Rosetta Stone, as it's now known, by two code-cracking scholars. One of them was a British scientist called Thomas Young and the other was a French Egyptologist and linguistic genius called Jean François Champollion. After much painstaking de-encrypting, Jean extended Thomas's earlier research by piecing together and making sense of the baffling hieroglyphic alphabet. And once *that* mystery was unravelled, it established a solid framework and basis for translating all those previously indecipherable documents!

Amongst *his* many breakthroughs, Thomas's most notable achievement was his realization that the hieroglyphs contained in the oval shapes (now known as cartouches) are the phonetically written personal logos of the Pharaohs. With this knowledge at their fingertips, Egyptologists would now be able to identify which tombful of treasure belonged to which Egyptian king. And it was recognizing the imprint of Tutankhamun's personal cartouche in the plaster on the wall that sealed the entrance to the tomb in the Valley of the Kings that led Howard Carter to realize he was on the threshold of an enormous breakthrough (in more ways than one!).

During the past 5,000 years the cartouche has become a worldwide symbol of long life, good luck and protection from evil. Egyptian cartouches were given their name by Napoleon's French soldiers because they were shaped like their own oval ammunition cartridges. But, as with all the other Egyptian kings, Tutankhamun would have known his personal nameplate not as his cartouche, but as his shenu, and would have no doubt been deeply offended by its new name!

# A message from the past

Dear future subject of the mighty Egyptian empire
What you see before you is my shenu. However,
my prophets inform me that you (in your profound
and hopeless ignorance) may know it as a
cartouche. It is my personal logo, kingly stamp,
nameplate, coat of arms, call it what you will (but
please, not cartouche!). Do you have a shenu? And
if you do is it as lovely and awe-inspiring as
mine? I very much doubt it!

The oval ring encircling my name represents a
length of magic rope which:

a) indicates the name it contains is that of one who is divine and rules the entire world, ie. yours truly!
b) will protect me from evil both while I live and in the Afterlife.

The first symbol, the bread loaf, stands for the sound of 'T'.

The next, the quail, represents the sound of 'U'.

Now little ignoramus from the future, have you remembered what the bread loaf symbol stands for? I thought not. Well, it's the sound of a T! So, if it's not beyond your limited abilities, little dimwit, put them all together! And what do you get? Yes, TUT, my first name.

Now this next one is called an 'ankh'. It represents a sandal strap. It is the symbol for 'life' or 'living'. It's followed by the pictogram for a reed (for the sound of 'i' or 'e'), a mat and finally water, representing the letter 'N'. Combined, these hieroglyphs spell 'Amun', the name of our most respected god (who also happens to be a personal friend, I'll have you know!). Put them all together and you end up with my whole name: Tut ankh amun which of course means, The living image of Amun! Is that sophisticated, or what?

But young Tut's life wouldn't have all been school, hieroglyphs and incredibly strict teachers. Some days would be filled with fun, excitement … and drama!

## SEE YOU LATER, REPTILE-HATER! IN THE NILE, CROCODILE!

### TUTANKHAMUN'S SECRET LOST PAPYRI DIARI

1336 BC Very, very hot today! So we went swimming in the Nile - in the shallow water, making sure we stayed away from the thick reed beds where crocodiles might be lurking.

'Now, much-respected, holy and special royal family children!' said our chief bodyguard 'Enjoy yourselves in the water. But do not go too deep. And be on the look out for those pesky crocodiles. Not to mention the terrible Nile catfish, that can kill you with one jab of their spine!'

So, as us royal kids played in the water, watched over by our bodyguards,

500 cubits* upriver from us, a group of peasant boys set about driving their cattle across the ford, all the while making a great racket and chanting magic incantations to keep the crocodiles and catfish away.

We had only been in the water a short while when there was a hullabaloo with lots of screaming and splashing.

'Oh no!' I thought as I ran out of the water as fast as my legs would carry me. 'A blinking crocodile must have got hold of one of my sisters!'

But then I looked towards the ford and saw that an enormous crocodile had seized one of the cows in its huge jaws and was thrashing the bellowing animal this way and that! But worse was to follow! As I watched in horror, a second crocodile did a great leap of at least ten cubits and seized one of the peasant boys in its fearsome jaws as he tried to run to safety. As the boy screamed with agony and terror the

*A cubit is the name for a measure of length used in ancient societies – it's about 45 cm long.

creature spun over and over in the water and the Nile turned red with that poor lad's blood. And finally it held him beneath the water and commenced to tear up his body with its savage jaws. I am so glad I was not born a peasant.

BURP!

## Crocs in a box

Crocodiles played an important part in the lives (and deaths) of many Egyptians. Thousands of mummified ones were discovered in ancient temples and several tomb scenes show those horrid crocs grabbing newborn hippopotamuses and gobbling them up. And hundreds of live ones were kept in several of the moats that surrounded their forts.

The Egyptians both hunted and worshipped crocodiles, but which they did may have depended on who happened to have the upper hand.

TAKE THAT, REPTILIAN VERMIN!

THOK!

INCIDENTALLY, DID YOU KNOW THAT I HAPPEN TO WORSHIP AND IDOLIZE YOU?

CHOMP!

King Tut actually ended up with at least one crocodile in his tomb. Or to be precise, a crocodile that thought it was a lioness ... with hippo-like tendencies! It was the goddess Ammut who, with her hippo's head, lion's legs and croc's tail appears as a couple of carvings on one of the ceremonial couches found in Tut's tomb. However, in other incarnations, Ammut had a crocodile's head and was generally known as 'female devourer of the dead'.

## TUTANKHAMUN'S SECRET LOST PAPYRI DIARI

**1336 BC** What an exciting day! We had a new creature delivered to the Royal Menagerie! We heard it before we saw it. Deafening roars echoed around the palace gardens, causing the parrots to squawk, the bears to growl, the baboons to bark and the giraffe and zebra to prick up their ears and prepare to flee.

Now I saw the cause of all this commotion. Coming through the gates of the royal palace were 12 enormous Nubians. Behind them they were pulling a cage containing a massive yellow cat. It was gripping the bars of the cage with its fangs and pulling at them, as if it wished to tear them away then hurl itself upon us, ripping us to shreds. And, just in case this should happen, ten of our bravest spearmen and archers stood by, their weapons at the ready.

The giant head was covered in tawny hair like a wig. It also had a long tasselled tail which it thrashed this way and that. The cat is called a lion.

After looking at it for some minutes, the Head Keeper of our Royal Menagerie pronounced himself satisfied.

A few days later: The lion is a lot quieter now. This may be because the royal vet has put a muzzle on him and also pulled out his claws! I think he must be missing them.

Two weeks later: Today the lion was let out of his cage and allowed to walk around the royal gardens. It was quite a scary thing to see, but we are in no danger because he is clawless and muzzled. Maybe one day I will make friends with him and he will be my pet.

## Tut's massive mouse-catcher

Being rich and idle and having everything that money could buy, it was inevitable that wealthy Egyptians would

want some really extreme pets to show off to their friends and keep them entertained on long hot afternoons. Not to mention accompanying them on their frequent hunting expeditions.

And, of course, the Egyptians with the most exotic pets were the Pharaohs. However, it wasn't always possible for the kings of the later dynasties to pop out and nab the odd lion, leopard, bear, rhino or cheetah for their private zoos. Mainly because their ancestors had more or less exterminated the lot! For instance, the Egyptian lion population had been just about wiped out by 1100 BC, possibly due to the efforts of Tut's grandad, Amenhotep III. Hieroglyphic artwork shows him killing more than 100 lions during a single hunt. So what the kings did was to exact their posh pets as part of the 'tribute' that the countries they'd conquered had to make to them on a regular basis.

Tutankhamun probably had at least one pet lion. In 2004, archaeologists investigating the tomb of Maia, his wet nurse, discovered a preserved lion skeleton in the area of the tomb dedicated to the cat goddess Bastet. It lay alongside vast quantities of bones of humans and animals, including masses of cats. After examining the skeleton, the archeologists concluded that the worn condition of the bones and teeth suggest the lion lived to an old age and was kept in captivity.

## Ankhkheprure Smenkhkaredjerkhepru

(or, anyone fancy a game of hieroglyph scrabble?)

In 1336 BC, when Tutankhamun was seven, his dad, Akhenaten, died. When this happened the kingship of Egypt was taken over by a mysterious individual known as Ankhkheprure Smenkhkaredjerkhepru ('Nobby', to his friends). Some people think that 'Nobby' was Akhenaten's brother, while others think he was Tutankhamun's brother. And others believe him to have been Queen Nefertiti pretending to be a man! However, and far more to the point, 'Nobby's' reign was short, and a couple of years later, he too, popped his sandals, leaving the way clear for Tutankhamun (or Tutankhaten as he was then known) to become king of all Egypt, at the grand old age of nine!

KING TUTANKHAMUN – *RULER*
OF EVERY SUBJECT UNDER
THE SUN!

# The Re

Egypt's Best-Selling Daily Papyrus

# TUTANKHAMUN
# CROWNED KING OF
# ALL EGYPT – AGED NINE!

**Writes Our Palace Correspondent: Reed Stalk**

What a difference a few days make! Only a week ago he was playing with his toy soldiers and chariots. Today, nine-year-old Tutankhamun is ruler of all Egypt, commander of the mighty Egyptian army and the living embodiment of a god!

Last week the boy and his wife, his half-sister, Ankhesenpaaten, sailed from their father's dream city of Akhetaten to Thebes for his coronation. As the splendid golden royal barge made its passage along the mighty Nile, crowds of curious peasants lined the banks anxious for a glimpse of the little couple who would soon be their divine rulers.

Arriving at Thebes, the soon-to-be-king-and-god and his little queen were taken to the palace of their grandfather, Amenhotep III, the place where their head-in-the clouds, new-age dreamer dad, Akhenaten, aka Amenhotep IV, had grown up. Then came the coronation.

As thousands of priests thronged the courtyard of the vast Karnak Temple, chanting from their papyri song-sheets and waving their incense burners, the children led a great procession of dignitaries and holy men through its massive gates and past the statues of their great ancestors: Tuthmosis I and Queen Hatshepsut. Now, perched on his special 'mini-throne', little Tut was presented with his crowns of kingship. Then, after taking his symbols of authority, his crook and flail, Tut was given his royal names: King of Upper and Lower Egypt, Strong Bull, The Lordly Manifestation of Re, He Who Displays the Regalia, The Living Image of Amun and He Who Calms the Two Lands. I just hope he can remember them all!

He was now officially the Pharaoh of all Egypt. As he and his little queen led the procession back to the palace for the coronation banquet they were cheered to the skies. Now, the good people of Thebes have a hope of returning to the good old days of 'pick-your-own god' religion. To heck with all this one-god-only nonsense is what we say at The Re! Tonight there will be unlimited feasting and revelry, with much wine and beer being consumed by the happy Thebans. And I for one will be joining them.

And finally, I must say this in young Tut's favour. Throughout that long hot coronation ceremony, only once did our esteemed new leader stifle a yawn. And only twice did he reach under his royal robes to give his royal bottom a really good royal scratch.

# Tut's crowning glories

As with most other ancient (and not so ancient) societies, wearing crowns and all sorts of other bizarre headgear meant an awful lot in the Egypt of 3,000 years ago. Becoming Pharaoh entitled Tut to sport all manner of fancy headwear, each item symbolizing at least one of his many responsibilities as top-Egyptian-banana.

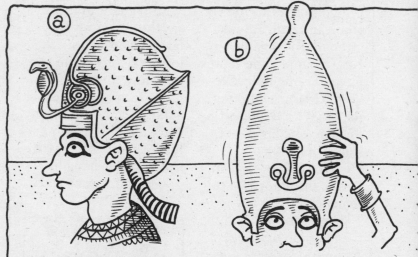

a) **Khepresh** This is Tut's bright-blue flanged crown-come-war helmet. It indicates his importance as a warrior king. The helmet is made out of leather and decorated with golden discs, and a cobra and a vulture – the two fearsome creatures that traditionally protected all the Egyptian Pharaohs.

b) **Hedjet** Despite its name this spectacular bit of skull-froth has nothing to do with airborne superheroes. It is the tall conical White Crown that indicated that Tutankhamun was king of Upper Egypt. Tut would have worn this as his main day-to-day crown (e.g. while he was putting the cat out or doing a bit of gardening) and also while he was present at ceremonies.

## King Tut's crook and flail

The other symbolic items that Tut was given at his coronation were his crook and flail, or in his case his mini-crook and mini-flail. Both big  and small ones were found in his tomb. The crook symbolically represented him as a shepherd who was sworn to look after the well-being of all his people. The flail indicated that he was a fearsome ruler who would smite his enemies at the least hint of provocation (just as soon as someone had explained to him what 'smite' meant).

**c) Deshret** This red, chair-shaped crown indicated that Tut was ruler of Lower Egypt. Gods and goddesses also wore deshrets, but without the cobra. Tut would mainly wear his deshret to really important ceremonies (he would certainly never be seen wearing it to do the dishes).

**d)** Tutankhamun's best-known bit of head-waffle is his **nemes**, because a gold metal and blue glass one forms part of his world-famous death mask. Technically speaking, it's not really a crown, but an elaborate fabric headdress. Nevertheless, nemes were only worn by Pharaohs. The nemes consists of a piece of striped cloth pulled tight across the forehead and tied into a tail at the back, leaving two dangly bits hanging down each side of the face. And, of course, the brow is decorated with the ever-present cobra and vulture.

So, what with the names and the crown-wearing and the shepherding and the smiting, not to mention being the earthly incarnation of a top god, all of a sudden the little lad had rather a lot on his plate. And getting to grips with the responsibilities associated with being the leader of a world superpower isn't the sort of thing you can knock off on a wet Tuesday afternoon, especially when you're only nine.

Consequently, and quite sensibly, when young Tut was made Pharaoh he wasn't left to get on with ruling Egypt all on his own. If he'd been allowed to do that he would have probably just banned school, had the teachers locked up and made sweets free for all children, then gone back to playing with his spinning top.

He received help and guidance from a team of top 'advisers', who were experienced in all matters relating to government. Things like making laws, collecting taxes, ensuring that the harvest was brought in successfully, organizing invasions of foreign countries, commissioning the construction of new roads and buildings (and making sure the bins got emptied on Thursdays).

And, of course, being both politicians *and* grown-ups, these various consultants quite naturally took advantage of their position and power to arrange things so that their own lives were extremely comfortable and privileged, possibly even *exploiting* Tut's immaturity and lack of experience!

For instance, Tut's advisers quickly set about restoring the old 'multi-god' religion, making Thebes the capital city again, giving the sacked priests their jobs back and arranging to have the groovy new-age city of Akhetaten reduced to rubble.

So let's meet a few of these movers and shakers and 'fat cats' who had such a profound influence and control over young Tut's life.

## King Tut's significant others

### Aye

**Claims to fame:** Aye was already a top official at the court of Tut's dad, Akhenaten. And his wife, Tey, was the wet-nurse of Nefertiti – Tut's dad's *other* number-one wife. Akhenaten gave them both gold collars for good service. Some people even think that Aye was Nefertiti's dad! And if that *was* the case, that would make him the grandad of Tut's wife, Ankhesenamun. But not only her grandad, but also her *husband*! Because a bit later on he got married to her. Yes, it all makes you want to go…

59

Amongst his other royal responsibilities Aye was Vizier (senior adviser), Fan Bearer on the Right Hand of the King (he was obviously extremely small), Overseer of all the Horses of His Majesty *and* The Royal Scribe! What with all that *and* the hanky-panky, it makes you wonder how he found the time!

He was also an old pal of Tut's granddad, Amenhotep III. This is what the (shy and retiring) Aye said about his relationship with Tut's grandpa.

> *I was favoured by his great lord every day great in favour from year to year because of the exceeding greatness of my excellence in my opinions. He doubled for me my favours like the number of sand: my name has penetrated into the palace because of my usefulness to the king.*

### Horemheb

Horemheb didn't have a drop of royal blood in his veins, but was a dab hand at soldiering and began his military career during Tut's dad's reign. While Akhenaten was faffing around with his new-fangled one-god religion and neglecting important jobs such as terrorizing the neighbours and demanding tribute (or protection money, as it's now called), it was General Horemheb who sustained Egypt's dominance over their conquered territories. And when little Tut took the throne he continued to do so.

## And some of the others

NB : Just one of these is not true – bet you can't spot it.

*Ipay*: Royal butler.

*Ipi*: Royal Scribe, Fan Bearer on the Right of Tutankhamun and Great Overseer of the Royal Household.

*Skipi*: Keeper of the Royal Kangaroos.

*Maia*: Tut's old wet nurse.

*Pa-atenemheb*: another royal butler

*Pay*: Overseer of the King's Private Apartments and the cattle of Amun (however, it's not thought that they actually kept the cattle in the apartments).

*Sennedjem and Senked*: overseers of tutors and nurses.

*Huy*: Viceroy of Nubia, a province of Egypt.

*Huy's wife Taemwadjsy*: Superior of Tutankhamun's Harem, i.e. the place where Egyptian kings kept their spare girlfriends.

*Maya*: Royal Treasurer (also in charge of Tut's pocket money).

*Pentu*: Vizier (we know that from inscription on a wine jar in Tut's tomb).

*Paramesse*: General who later served as Vizier under Pharaoh Horemheb (yes, he finally landed the big one!). When Horemheb died he took the throne as Ramses I.

**Important Tut-note**

Unlike a lot of the other Egyptian Pharaohs, hardly anything is actually known about the significant events that took place during Tutankhamun's life. This is mainly due to the fact that, despite being full to bursting with treasures, his tomb contained hardly any written information about him. Consequently, archaeologists and Egyptologists have only pieced together a *very* sketchy picture of his life and times, basing their detective work on the objects, pictures of him and hieroglyphic references to him discovered both in his and other Pharaohs' tombs.

However, one thing we can be certain of is that while Tut's numerous helpers were busy running the show, he would have carried on with his education and would also be fulfilling his numerous kingly duties by appearing in all his royal finery at religious and state ceremonies. And, naturally, as he grew up, his tastes and interests would change. He would soon cast aside his childhood toys and during his teenage (and final) years, be taking part in more adult and challenging sports and pastimes. Sports and pastimes that may well have led to his early death!

## CHARIOTS OF DESIRE

### TUTANKHAMUN'S SECRET LOST PAPYRI DIARI

1325 BC Today I have had an extremely eventful, exciting, exhausting, not to mention excruciatingly painful, day! For I led the Royal Hunt, splendid and awe-inspiring in my leopard-skin tunic, quilted kilt, silver apron and driving my magnificent new golden chariot!

With the exception of lovely dancing girls, banqueting, my wife, Ankhesenamun, music, good wine, fine clothes and the exquisite objects of art with which I am constantly surrounded, I really can't think of anything I love better than hunting! Apart from my divine and exalted self, of course!

As Re once more rose from the Underworld, my grooms led my magnificent chariot horses from the royal stables, neighing and tossing their heads this way and that so that their head-plumes shimmered and flickered in the early morning sunlight. Then, as they stamped and snorted, impatient to be off, their chestnut coats all glossy, the grooms harnessed them to my gorgeous golden chariot. Now I mounted my glittering conveyance and summoned my favourite hunting dog, a magnificent beast, a king amongst dogs, who, unknownst to me just then, would soon be laying down his life for me!

Seizing the reins, I gave a click of my tongue and the hooves of my horses were pounding the limestone pavements of Thebes with my hounds following in full cry, as they anticipated the sport to come. We were, of course, accompanied by my swift-footed bodyguards running alongside me, clutching their bows and spears. They, in turn, were followed by the royal huntsmen aboard their chariots (which weren't nearly so magnificent as mine!) and the royal physician carrying his medical bag, packed with healing meat, milk, lint, honey and roast mouse. And finally, came our servants and slaves, driving the donkeys which were laden with the food, drink and spare weaponry, which would make our day a successful one.

As we charged through the city gates, all around, my adoring subjects ceased their brewing, baking, bartering and building, to stare at me in wonder, awestruck by the beauty and wondrousness of the sight they beheld, no doubt hardly believing their amazing good fortune to find themselves in the presence of someone so god-like, so uniquely wonderful and perfect, as I! (To be continued.)

# Cool wheels

When Howard Carter opened up Tut's tomb, he discovered six magnificent chariots. Each of them had originally been taken to pieces by Tut's 'kwik-flit' un-fitters, so that it could be carried along the narrow corridor to his tomb. Then its component parts had been neatly stored away in readiness for use in Tut's afterlife (his servants presumably being dab hands at reassembling flat-pack chariots). However, after untidy grave robbers had done their stuff back in 1000 BC, what Howard came across was more like a chariot scrapyard, filled with a great jumble of mangled and mouldering bits and pieces of chariot. Nevertheless, determined and dedicated engineers and Egyptologists eventually set about disentangling the jumbled-up nightmare and, after sorting the pieces of the six 'chariot jigsaws', they set about slowly and painstakingly identifying what went with what, then rebuilding five of the six chariots.

And when awestruck modern motoring engineers examined the reassembled chariots, they quickly came to the conclusion that these high-performance, Pharaoh-a-go-go machines were miracles of ancient sports-chariot engineering, displaying sophistication and design features that matched, and in some cases, actually outclassed, those of modern vehicles! For instance…

**a)** On examining the wheel spokes and joints of the chariots, the engineers discovered that they could cope with the sort of forces, knocks and scrapes that modern aeroplanes are designed to withstand.

**b)** The chariots' 3,000-year-old lightweight wheels were more advanced and better designed than the wooden ones used on veteran cars of the early 20th century!

**c)** the chariots' sophisticated suspension system used a complex sub-assembly of springs and dampers made from the best materials available. This resulted in unsurpassed structural dynamics and ride quality. Or, to put it another way, you didn't lose your lunch when it went over a bump!

**d)** It soon became obvious that it could not have been developed without being subjected to the sort of experimental modelling, pushing-it-beyond-its-limits racing-circuit and test-track research and analysis now associated with high-performance sports cars.

**e)** Even with the aid of computers and 3,000 years of accumulated technical knowledge, the engineers still couldn't improve on the way the chariot had been designed and assembled.

# Tut's pocket-rocket

WHEELS AND CHASSIS ALL SHAPED BY USING UP-TO-THE-MINUTE STEAM-BENDING TECHNOLOGY

LINKS MADE FROM BONE, STONE AND COPPER ALLOY USED TO ATTACH THE HORSES' HARNESSES TO THE CHARIOT

GORGEOUS DECORATIVE INTERIOR INLAY MADE FROM GYPSUM PLASTER, FAÏENCE AND GLASS

COOL!

THONGS, HARNESSES, TYRES, HORSE BLINKERS AND TRACES - LEATHER AND RAWHIDE

MATTING AND KICKBOARDS MADE FROM FINEST TEXTILES

LIGHT AND STRONG FRAMEWORK MADE FROM WOOD SUCH AS ASH AND BIRCH

QUIVERS OF ARROWS AND SMALL POINTED SPEARS STRAPPED TO THE INSIDE OF 'COCKPIT'

'COCKPIT' PLATFORM 75cm ABOVE THE GROUND - MADE FROM TOUGH LEATHER WHICH ACTS AS A SHOCK ABSORBER, CUSHIONING THE RIDERS FROM JOLTS AND VIBRATIONS

'COCKPIT' OPEN AT THE BACK, SO CREW CAN GET IN AND OUT REALLY QUICKLY, ESPECIALLY IN EMERGENCIES

Woo! NICE WHEELS!

SPOKES: MADE BY BENDING PIECES OF WOOD INTO V SHAPES GLUED TOGETHER TO FORM A HEXAGONAL STAR

TIPS OF V'S FASTENED TO HUB WITH WET COW GUTS THAT GO ROCK HARD WHEN THEY DRY

LIGHTWEIGHT WHEELS WITH STRONG SPOKES ATTACHED TO A CENTRAL HUB

# TUTANKHAMUN'S SECRET LOST PAPYRI DIARI

1325 BC (continued)

Soon my hunting party left the city behind, then, having passed the great mortuary temples and tombs of my illustrious ancestors, we were galloping across the desert plains where we knew we would find gazelle, antelope, deer and ostrich aplenty. And, with luck, hyena, leopard and jackal! Now we slowed to a canter, as my chief scout, trotting some 500 cubits ahead of us, raised his hand in warning. For he had spied a group of ostriches gathered at a waterhole. Sensing our presence, the keen-eared and sharp-eyed birds fell to the ground, spreading themselves flat in dust in the hope that we might mistake them for mounds of earth in the shimmering heat haze. We had them at our mercy! They were sitting ducks! Well, sitting ostriches, actually! But then, one of our pack-

donkeys reared and screamed in
agony, as a great horned viper,
more than 15 cubits long, rasped
in anger, unleashed its coils and
leapt at the poor animal, fangs
bared.

But we paid it no heed, for
the ostriches were now galloping
across the sand as fast as
their long legs would carry
them, running straight towards
a steep-sided canyon, which we
knew to be a dead end.

I tied the reins of my chariot
horses around my waist, seized
my bow, nocked an
arrow and giving a
great yell, set my
steeds, hounds and
hunters in pursuit of
the birds. But then, as I
drew level with the fleeing
ostriches, there was a terrible
splintering sound! In the next
moment, my chariot had flipped
on to its side and I was flying
through the air. I hit the ground
with a great thud. As I did I
heard a sickening 'crack!', feeling
an agonizing pain shoot along
through my left thigh. But this

was only the beginning of my troubles. For I was still attached to the reins of my horses, which had now broken away from my chariot. No doubt terrified by my screams of pain, they thundered across the open desert, following the fleeing ostriches, dragging me over the ground and leaving my bodyguards far behind.

Soon we had entered the impassable canyon and I found myself in among at least 30 of the birds, all of them mad with fear and panic. As my horses drew to a halt, the biggest ostrich rushed at me, intent on ripping me from end to end with its lethal claw. But as it did, there was a great barking and growling. Next moment, my beloved lead hunting dog was hurling himself at the enraged beast. The ostrich struck and its terrible weapon did its worst! But it was not I who was the victim. It was my dog! The bird's huge claw ripped open his stomach from end to end and in an instant my beloved dog was yelping in agony. Moments later, as my bodyguards finally arrived and set about slaughtering the murderous ostrich and his screeching wives, my dog gave a great shudder and died in my arms.

So my day was ruined by this tragedy. Tomorrow, as the mummy makers set about preparing the good hound for the next world, I will have the royal barber shave off my eyebrows as a mark of my respect for my pet and to show everyone that I am now in mourning for this wonderful animal.

## TUTANKHAMUN'S SECRET LOST PAPYRI DIARI

1324 BC Today I am feeling sad, pained, puzzled and perplexed. I am sad because I miss my beloved hunting hound, even though it is so long since his doggy-mummy was laid in the tomb, alongside all my other long-dead pets.

I am pained because my thigh, broken in that hunting accident, is still not better. The royal physicians did all they could, wrapping it with raw meat, anointing it with oil and honey and chanting their magic spells. But still, almost one year on, it gives me pain. And on some days, like today, I feel sick and dizzy and a most putrid smell leaks from the rotten part, despite the efforts of the flesh-eating maggots that were applied by the physicians.

WRIGGLE

BB WRIGGLE

I am puzzled because I am thinking back to my chariot crash. It should not have happened! That chariot had been tested and tested, time and time again in the worst conditions possible, and had been proved capable of standing up to all sorts of knocks. So why would one of the wheels suddenly shear off without warning? I can only think it had been sabotaged. But who would do such a thing?

And finally, I am perplexed because my advisers are acting very strangely! Going off into corners to whisper to each other, giving me odd looks, rubbing their hands gleefully, as if they are anticipating coming into great wealth, or even more power than they have already. Which, in fact, is the reverse of what will soon happen. For in a few weeks, it will be my 19th birthday and I will no longer need their services. I will have total power over all Egypt. I will make all of the decisions that affect my people and my land.

And then things will change around here! As I've grown up I've realized that Aye and Horemheb have been taking advantage of me, introducing new laws and practices that are not at all to my liking! So there's going to be a shake-up! I am even thinking of bringing back my father's one-god worship.

Now I must stop writing for I feel quite exhausted and desperate for sleep. But what's that? I hear footsteps outside my room. Who can it be at this late hour?

And that's the last we'll hear from Tut. As we now know, he died at somewhere around the age of 19. Whether he was murdered, died from his broken leg, or simply became a victim of one of the plagues that occasionally struck Egypt, no one's sure. However, as far as he and his pals were concerned this was most definitely *not* the end. In fact, it was the beginning!

Because, once Tut had been suitably gift-wrapped and tucked up in his tomb, he would begin his journey to the Afterworld, where he would be judged by the gods, who would then decide whether he was worthy of a place in heaven – or hell! And because he was a Pharaoh (and therefore part-god), the outcome of the judgement was more or less a foregone conclusion. He would most definitely go to Paradise.

But we're getting ahead of ourselves. We can't send him off yet. He's got to be made presentable in preparation for his big leaving party! And the only people who can do that are those ancient Egyptian shrink-wrappers and mummy's boys, the embalmers!

# AND WE ALL LIVED HAPPILY EVER AFTER!

Like every ancient Egyptian, Tut wanted to live for ever. And, because he and his pals believed the body was the home of their soul or spirit, the last thing they wanted was for it to be destroyed, or turned into a heap of manky putrefying flesh by those pesky bacteria!

**CHOMP CHOMP!**

**NOSH NOSH!**

Because if *that* happened, their spirit would have nowhere to rest and would go floating off, to be lost for ever! You see, the thing is, what with it being completely invisible, once your spirit does go absent without leave, you don't stand a catacomb in hell's chance of finding it! So, what was needed was an everlasting body, where the spirit would remain safe for all eternity! In other words, the thing we now call a mummy!

**IT'S A WRAP!**

# A short history of ancient-Egyptian embalming

Free-range mummies: The earliest Egyptians simply bunged their dead pals in desert pits, then covered them with sand and rocks to prevent the wild animals from eating them (and to stop them climbing out again).

It's bacteria that cause things to decay and bacteria like moist conditions. But in Egypt it hardly ever rains. So, for starters, the extremely dry sandpits were no-go zones for the bacteria! In addition to which, the hot air and dry sand dehydrated (dried out) the bodies quickly, leaving them looking much as they had in life (if slightly less active and a whole lot wrinklier).

If you want to see one of these 'natural' mummies 'in the flesh', there's one in the British Museum in London. Despite the fact that he's 5,500 years old, he's still got all his bits and pieces, including his red hair! The staff nicknamed him Ginger.

In time, the Egyptians became more protective of their dead and began putting them in coffins to safeguard them from desert scavengers such as jackals and vultures. However, on opening the coffins they were horrified to discover that the bodies had rotted away. The atmosphere inside the coffins, not being exposed to the drying wind and sand, had become damp, providing a perfect environment for the bacteria.

Something had to be done! So, as the centuries ticked by, smarter Egyptians weighed up the facts and, by trial and error, came up with the preservation technique that we now call mummification. By the time our golden boy checked out, mummification was a high-tech state-of-the-art body-preservation technique. The lad couldn't have been in better hands!

Which is why he still manages to turn up for his final, farewell, comeback-tour autopsy gigs still looking like he's just walked out of the keep-fit centre (well, almost!).

# The shrink-wrapping of King Tutankhamun
## A step-by-step account

As carried out by royal mummifier and his trainee embalmers

**Time taken:** 70 days

**Materials used:** Water, palm wine, linen, perfume, salt, bling fit for a king (preferably oodles of it!)

**Where it takes place:** our specially designated Egyptian 'Good' house. Or an open tent, situated well away from picnic areas and pavement cafes.

**Special skills needed:**

1) Knowledge of the magic incantations to be recited at the various stages of this makeover-to-end-all-makeovers.

2) A thorough understanding of the assorted bits and bobs that make up the human anatomy and where to find them.

## Step one – Removing the squidgy bits

Having first made sure our king is completely dead, we whip out our esteemed client's innards. They go rotten very quickly, so we need to do this fast! To reach them, we make a four-inch cut in the left side of the abdomen, then…

Right, stick your mitt in and have a good feel around. Got anything? You have? Good! No of course it's not a 'big wiggly snake'! How would one of those have got in there? It's His Majesty's blinking intestines. OK, pull them out! Yes, never-ending, aren't they? Now for his stomach, lungs and liver. But leave the heart in. He'll need that for the Afterworld.

Well done, that's everything out then. All you need to do now is give all these bits and pieces a wash in palm wine then… Oh dear! You shouldn't have done that! Licking your fingers really isn't a good idea whilst you're eviscerating.

OK! Now for that utterly useless organ, the brain. To debrain our ex-monarch, we stick our special debraining tool up the nose. No, not *your own* nose! *King Tut's* nose! Now break the bone that separates the nose from the brain, then give it a good old wiggle. Keep doing this until the brain is mashed up into pieces small enough to pull down the nostrils. When you've hooked them all out, throw them away.

81

## Step two – Drying out the body and squidgy bits

We must now thoroughly dry our king's body.

No, not like that, you ancient Egyptian nitwits! We do this using…

### Natron: nature's little desiccater

We use white crystals known as natron for desiccating (drying out) dead bodies. Put quite simply, natron is salt. However, if you want get all scientific…

NATRON IS A MIXTURE OF SODIUM BICARBONATE AND HYDRATED SODIUM BICARBONATE, PLUS SMALLER QUANTITIES OF SODIUM CHLORIDE AND SODIUM SULFATE

A SCIENCE TEACHER

I'VE JUST LOST THE WILL TO LIVE!

ME TOO!

It draws out every last bit of moisture, very, very efficiently! But, in addition to this, natron does something else. Whenever it comes into contact with moisture, the amount of acid in it increases! And that acid wipes out those pesky bacteria that like nothing better than turning dead Pharaohs into dollops of stinking, putrefying flesh!

So natron is perfect for mummifying. And what's more, we've got tons of the stuff lying around in our dried-up lake beds, all there for the taking! So it's no wonder that drying out and wrapping dead bodies has become such a big business in ancient Egypt, rather than the Amazonian rainforest.

### Step three – Drip-drying King Tutankhamun

First we fill our empty Pharaoh with linen packets containing natron. Next, we put him in a big stone tray and cover him completely with finely ground natron. Now that we've thoroughly a'salted our Pharaoh, we must leave him to 'mature' for 40 days. No, of course you can't add a sprig of parsley and stick a clove of garlic on him. You're preparing a mummy, not Sunday lunch!

## Step four – Drying his squidgy bits

We dry out our client's liver, stomach, intestines, and lungs by individually wrapping them in linen covered with natron, then storing them in specially designed 'Canopic' jars. We can't use any old jars, or we might find ourselves in trouble.

### The Canopic jars
The Canopic jars, which we put the organs in, are made in the image of the children of our god, Horus. So we put:

The liver ... in the human-headed god known as Imsety.
The stomach ... in the jackal-headed god known as Duamutef.
The intestines ... in the falcon-headed god known as Qebehsenuef.
The lungs ... in the baboon-headed god known as Hapy.

AND FINALLY, THE **BRAIN** IN THE REALLY-TINY BEARDED GOD KNOWN AS **DOPEY!**

NB One of these is not true.

## Step five – Preparing the body for wrapping

We remove the natron packets from the abdomen and close the hole. We do this by covering it with a flattish piece of gold called a tablet. We wash the natron off the body with palm wine.

Now that we've removed the internal organs, we've noticed that some areas of our king have gone a bit droopy, or collapsed completely. To make his mummy as lifelike as possible, we're going stuff these areas with linen or sawdust.

What with human eyes being mostly liquid, we notice that the natron's had a rather distressing effect on King Tut's peepers. So we replace them with false ones made from black and white stone.

We now note that King Tut has a problem with 'dry' skin. We don't want him turning up in the Fields of Paradise looking like a tortoise's great-grandma, so we anoint his entire body with perfumed oils to remoisten his skin and remove those unsightly wrinkles.

We next anoint our Pharaoh with divine-smelling spices and fragrances such as cinnamon and myrrh.

We also find that one or two of the king's fingernails and toenails have dropped off during the drying-out period, so tie we them back on with bits of string.

### Step six – And now to 'gift-wrapping' our Pharaoh

We'll be using lots of linen for this – possibly as much as 700 square metres! We start with his pinkies and his Tut tootsies, wrapping each one individually.

THIS LITTLE PIGGY WENT TO MEMPHIS

THIS LITTLE PIGGY WENT HOME...

All right, that's quite enough of that! Just get on with wrapping the feet and hands. We also slide golden sheaths on to each of his fingers before we wrap them.

Now for the main body. For this we carefully wind the long strips of linen around and around it. And as we wrap, we stash loads of really high-class jewellery between the bandages. It's there so Pharaoh Tut will have a safe journey through the Underworld.

NOT TO MENTION HAVING PLENTY OF 'READIES' FOR BRIBES AND TIPS...

... BENT GATEKEEPERS, THAT SORT OF THING.

WINK WINK

TAP TAP

Most importantly of all, we place a scarab beetle charm over King Tut's heart. It will protect it and stop it blabbing about any little 'indiscretions' he's committed down here on Earth, e.g. overdue library books, that sort of thing.

As we're wrapping and stashing we also slap several coats of resin on the bandages to keep them in place and preserve them. And we write magic spells and invocations (wishes) on his bandages.

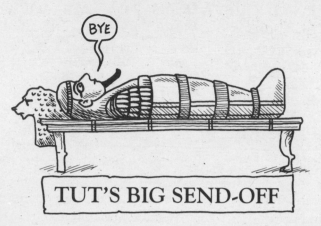

# TUT'S BIG SEND-OFF

Tut's funeral cortege prepares to leave the Royal Palace at Thebes. NB. Reader! One of the items in this illustration may not be entirely authentic – can you spot it?

CARTS AND SLEDGES STACKED HIGH WITH TREASURE GOODS AND FOOD FOR TUT'S AFTERLIFE – GOLDEN SWORDS AND DAGGERS, JEWELLERY, TRUMPETS OF BEATEN SILVER, GOLD AND GLASS OINTMENT POTS, TUT'S SCALED LEATHER ARMOUR, SWISS ARMY KNIFE...ETC.

LORDS, SENIOR CIVIL SERVANTS AND TOP ADVISERS, PRIESTS SPRINKLING DUST WITH MILK AND WATER, SQUADRONS OF WAR CHARIOTS PULLED BY BEAUTIFULLY PLUMED HORSES

PROFESSIONAL WOMEN MOURNERS WAILING, ULULATING, THROWING SAND OVER THEMSELVES AND TEARING CLOTHES

MUSICIANS PLAYING HARPS, LUTES AND FLUTES

SHAVEN-HEADED PRIESTS IN QUILTED LINEN KILTS, SOME WEARING PANTHER AND LEOPARD SKINS

BOWLS OF BURNING INCENSE AND WATER FOR THE CEREMONIAL PURIFICATION

STEADY ON! IT'S A FUNERAL, REMEMBER!

COUGH, SPLUTTER, COUGH!

# THE ENTOMBMENT OF TUTANKHAMUN

As reported by The Mourning Show on Radio Thebes
With pictographs by Arty Symbols

Just 70 days ago our beloved monarch was suddenly
snatched from this life in most tragic, not to mention
mysterious, and possibly suspicious, circumstances.
And now we have reached the ultimate moment. The
King is to depart for the Afterlife. Gathered before me
are the most important people in his life.

WAIL WAIL KEEN WAIL! OH MY BELOVED TUT, YOU WERE TOO YOUNG TO DIE!

FAREWELL, GREAT KING! MISSING YOU ALREADY!

I AM A CHILDLESS WIDOW-WOMAN, ALL ALONE IN THIS CRUEL WORLD. WITH ONLY CONNIVING CREEPS FOR COMPANY! WHATEVER WILL I DO?

TEE HEE! I'M GOING TO BE KING NOW!

SO SORRY YOU'RE GONE, KING TUT!

NOT!

ANKHESENAMUN: (TUT'S WIFE)

HOREMHEB: COMMANDER OF TUT'S ARMIES

AYE: PRINCIPAL ADVISER

Having crossed the glittering Nile and made our way to the Valley of the Kings, we are now gathered at the King's tomb for the final ceremony. The high priest is reading from his papyrus scroll, keen to ensure that the ceremony is carried out exactly as ancient scriptures dictate. The sights, smells and sounds are overwhelming: the glitter of gold, the wails of the women, the chanting of the priests, the brilliantly coloured ostrich-fan plumes drenched in heady perfumes, the pungent smoke coiling from the glowing incense cones, the reek of the dung dropped by the soon-to-be slaughtered animals, the acrid burning oil in the lamps, the slightly rancid smell of the milk with which the priests daub the king's mummified body.

And now, new notes are added to this symphony of smells, sights and sounds: screams of pain and the odour of freshly spilled blood! For the ritual killing of the bulls, ducks and gazelles has begun.

91

They roar, they bellow and they quack! And they
struggle. But to no avail! They are held down by
strong hands and the priest's knife quickly slits their
throats. The high priest now amputates the leg of the
largest bull. For it is time for the opening of the
mouth ceremony. Before Tutankhamun enters the
tomb for all eternity, his mouth must be ritually
'opened', so that he may breathe and recite the magic
spells from the Book of the Dead as he passes into the
Afterworld. A likeness of the king is used for this
ritual. Grand Vizier Aye raises his woodworker's adze
and touches the mouth of one of the guardian statues.
Next he touches it with the bull's leg. The mouth-
opening ritual over, mourners now descend the 16
steps to the burial chamber. The pall-bearers carry the
body to the stone sarcophagus, their lamps making
the animals and servants in the newly painted murals
appear to leap and dance, while the shadows of the
sculpted gods rear up eerily and menacingly on the
walls of the catacomb.

It's as if they are already carrying out their duties of guarding the Pharaoh's body! Inside the stone sarcophagus lie three coffins, one inside the other. As the priests lower Tutankhamun's body into the inner coffin the moaning and ululating of Ankhesenamun and the professional women mourners becomes almost unbearable.

It's time for the lid of the first coffin to be put in place. But not before the priests have anointed the body with perfumed oils and unguents. And we look upon the king for a final time. Never again will human beings see the face of King Tutankhamun. But now a small drama takes place! Just as the lid is being put in place, Ankhesenamun rushes forwards and attempts to throw herself on top of her husband! But she is restrained by priests and the lid is finally put in place. Still sobbing, Ankhesenamun places a flower wreath around the sculpted cobra.

Now the mourners ascend the steps from the tomb and workmen erect the three nesting shrines that will surround the sarcophagus. That done, the masons wall up the burial chamber and Tutankhamun's seals are impressed in the wet plaster.

But the day is not yet finished! For now Ankhesenamun and the palace officials will feast on sheep, four sorts of Nile duck, two plover and the finest wines from the Pharaoh's vineyards. When the meal is finished all the dishes, cups, leftovers, and even the little brushes that are used to sweep up will all be ritually buried, because they will otherwise defile King Tut's tomb! And jeopardize his journey to the Afterworld! So they must be buried close by. This also signifies that the funeral is over. So now, we must take our leave!

And that was that! King Tut was finally on his way to the World of the Dead. And, with a bit of luck, Paradise! But before he got to that final dream destination, he had one test to pass. His judgement in the Hall of Maat.

## The weighing of the heart

In order to get into ancient Egyptian heaven all you had to do was pass one big exam. But it wasn't the sort of exam you could simply last-minute-panic swot-up on the night before, then just scrape through by the skin of your teeth. Because it was a test you had been preparing for all your life! By doing your very best to be good!

# A 'Q-and-A' guide and some tips to help you through a *very* testing time

*Q: Where it will take place?*
**A:** The Judgement Room, also known as the Hall of Maat, somewhere in the Afterworld.

*Q: Who's going to be there?*
**A:** You (of course!) and a panel of 14 judges who will 'weigh up' your good and bad deeds. They will include Horus (the god of the sky), Thoth (scribe of the dead – he'll be taking notes), Anubis (the jackal god) and most importantly of all Maat (the goddess of truth and justice).

*Q: What will happen to me?*
**A:** The jackal god Anubis will lead you before the scales, then place your heart (which of course, contains your conscience) in one tray of the weighing scales and the feather of Maat in the other.

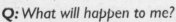

*Q: What will happen if my heart is heavier than the feather?*
A: Ha! It will be obvious to all present that your heart has been made heavy by your many evil deeds.

**Q:** *And will I be punished?*

**A:** Oh, yessss, most certainly! Ammit, the devourer of souls god, with his crocodile head and hippopotamus's legs, will immediately *eat* your heart, condemning you to hell, for ever and ever!

**Q:** *What will happen if the feather is heavier than my heart?*

**A:** It will indicate to one and all that you have led a righteous and good life. You will be presented to Osiris, who will lead you to the Fields of Paradise where you will live happily ever after!

**Q:** *But what will happen if I've been generally good, and only a teensy bit naughty?*

**A:** Don't worry too much about that. Anubis knows how hard it is to be perfect all of the time. So, if he decides you're a generally OK sort of dude, he'll make a few 'adjustments' to the scales, just so's you aren't condemned to hell for all time, simply because you once accidentally stood on an ant.

**Q:** *Is there any other way I can reduce my chances of being 'sent down'?*

**A:** Yes, there is! For a small down-payment and several thousand weekly contributions, you can purchase yourself a jewelled scarab ornament. All you have to do then is leave instructions for your embalmers to take out your real heart and replace it with the 'extremely light' scarab. No way will that go blabbing about your misdeeds. Your passage to heaven will be as good as guaranteed.

**Q:** *Just out of curiosity, whichever way I go, up or down, what will it be like when I get there?*

**A:** Read on and you will see!

# Ancient Egyptian heaven and hell
## Go to Paradise – Egyptian-style!

## PHOENIX AFTERLIFE ASSURANCE SERVICES
### By Appointment to His Majesty the Pharaoh

Dear King Tutankhamun,

Rest assured! With our exciting new 'Afterlife-Assured' Policy, you can look forward to an eternity of uninterrupted happiness. After you've died and been mummified and buried with all the trimmings and whatnot, you can look forward to an exciting new life in Paradise! Once there, you'll get to rub shoulders with all manner of heavenly superstars, including that pair of A-list celebrity gods, Re and Osiris. But of course, this only happens to those who've been very, very good here on Earth! However, in your case, Tutankhamun, King of Upper and Lower Egypt, Strong Bull, The Lordly Manifestation of Re, He Who Displays the Regalia, The Living Image of Amun, He Who Calms the Two Lands, Dynamic of Laws, Who Propitiates all the Gods, Fitting of Created Forms (and of course, without wishing to sound the slightest bit creepy) we have no doubt that you will enter Paradise! So, esteemed Pharaoh, here's a foretaste of what to expect...

**1)** First your body will rest in your tomb waiting for the sun to come up. But don't fret, King Tutankhamun, come up it will! Re is the most dependable of our gods! I mean, does the sun shine in Egypt, or does it not?

**2)** Then, when Re is finally reborn from the Underworld in the east (yes, that red-hot god really is a 'RE' of sunlight!), your soul will leave your tomb and join him and all those other non-stop party-people in Paradise.

**3)** Here, you will be welcomed by all those other talented, good-looking, wonderful, special, strong (and super-rich) people who have also popped their earthly sandals and entered Paradise.

**4)** And then, young Tut, it will be just fun, fun, fun, all the way! Chill out in idyllic green meadows, enjoy the wall-to-wall blue skies and cooling breezes, soak up the hot-but-not-too-hot sunshine (courtesy of Big Re, of course).

**5)** Listen, though, King Tut! You're going to find all this non-stop partying pretty tiring! But we've thought of that too! When night comes and Re disappears in the west, you will simply return to your mummified body, catch some ZZZZs and recharge your batteries! Then, when Re rises in the morning, the fun begins again! And it's all for ever and ever!

## Go to hell – Ancient Egyptian-style!

Dear Wrongdoer,

Oh dear! Don't know quite how to tell you this, but you've failed the feather test. When we weighed your heart, the scales didn't so much as dip, but they *disintegrated*! You … have been one baaaad dude! So, during your everlasting stay in Hell, or the 'Slaughtering Place' as we like to call it, expect most, or more possibly all, of the following. (Depends on how crabby the fierce goddess of the Underworld, Sekhmet, and her Demon Butchers are feeling!)

WHO'S BEEN A NAUGHTY BOY, THEN?

**1)** When you arrive the Demon Butchers (many of them ex-humans like yourself, hand-picked by Sekhmet for their viciousness) will pull off your mummy wrappings so that your body immediately begins to rot. Then, if they're feeling peckish, they'll tear out your insides and gobble them up whilst biting great chunks out of your flesh and washing the whole lot down with mouthfuls of your blood!

**2)** You'll not only be made to walk around on your head, but will also have your hands tied behind your back as you do! And for a change you'll occasionally be burned in ovens and boiled in cauldrons.

**3)** Shezmu, the god of the wine press, will use his grape-squidger to squeeze all the blood out of you and your fellow sinners. Then you'll all be made to swim about in the vast, blood-red lake it forms.

**4)** Your heart will be taken out and your soul will be separated from your body, forever unable to return to you. You'll even lose your shadow!

**5)** You'll have no air to breathe and constantly suffer from agonizing hunger and raging thirst.

**6)** And, of course, you'll live constantly in stinking darkness, never ever again getting the chance to enjoy that lovely stuff known as daylight and sunshine. Even though you wail and cry out to Re the great sun god, he will pass you by, abandoning you to the eternal night of the Underworld!

So that's about it then, have a really horrible time, you good-for-nothing you!

No, no! There is one other thing. Nearly forgot to mention this. Each day you'll be made to eat your own poo and drink your own wee.

Well, what did you expect … Disneyland? This is Hell, you know!

Bet you wish you'd been nicer to other people and worked harder at school!

Meanwhile back in the land of the living...

## A tale of death, duplicity and desperation

Tut's burial was by no means the end of his story. Poor Ankhesenamun must have been devastated by his early death. And to make matters worse, she and Tut had no royal children to carry on the family reign. The throne was now empty. The most powerful job in all Egypt was up for grabs. Now, 60-year-old Aye prepared to make his move. Anticipating his intentions, the terrified Ankhesenamun sent this letter to a Hittite king named Suppiluliumas.

*My husband has died and I have no son. They say about you that you have many sons. You might give me one of your sons to become my husband. Never shall I pick out a servant of mine and make him my husband...
I am afraid!*

Nothing like getting straight to the point, is there? The 'servant' who Ankhesenamun mentions in the letter is generally thought to have been Aye. But why *was* she afraid? Had she discovered that Aye had Tut bumped off? Or maybe both Aye and Horemheb had had him done in?

And then the plot thickened!

After reading the letter, King Suppiluliumas sent one of his advisers to check that this was a genuine request and not a treacherous trick. Then King Suppiluliumas sent his youngest son, Zanannza, to marry Ankhesenamun. However, as soon as Zanannza reached Egypt, he and his companions were all murdered! Ooer! Now Aye married Ankhesenamun and he became king. We know about their marriage because archaeologists found a blue-glass finger ring engraved with their names. But, not long after this, Ankhesenamun disappeared. Now that he was king, did Aye have her bumped off too? There is no reference to her in his tomb, only of his other wife Tey!

# PART TWO
# HOWARD CARTER'S REALLY
# BIG ADVENTURE

So, with one detective thriller still warm in its grave, we now move to another. The amazing tale of Howard Carter and his long search for Tutankhamun and his tombful of treasure. This is made all the more spine-tingling and terrifyingly tense by the blood-chilling mystery of the 'Curse of the Mummy!'

# HOWARD 'CART-IT-ALL-AWAY'

Howard Carter (or Howard 'Cart-It-All-Away', as some unkind people might prefer to call him) was born in Earl's Court in London in 1874. If it wasn't for Howard and his passion for all things ancient and Egyptian, not to mention his detective's instincts and his dogged determination to follow his dream, Tutankhamun and his tombful of treasure would most likely still be lying undisturbed and undiscovered beneath the sands of the Valley of the Kings.

Howard was the son of Samuel Carter, an artist who made his living by painting portraits of the furry friends of Norfolk toffs and bigwigs.

It was through his dad's connections with all these wealthy, worldly and wonderfully well-educated Victorians that Howard first came into contact with the astonishing old relics that would set him off on his 30-year quest to find an undiscovered Pharaoh's tomb.

Howard Carter's secret lost diaries
<u>1888</u> I am 14 years old and, today, Father is taking me to a very grand house called Didlington Hall. It is the home of some very wealthy and important people called Lord and Lady Amherst. Father paints pictures of their dogs and cats and racehorses. Lady Amherst is bonkers about archaeology and is forever nipping off to Egypt and fossicking about there.

<u>Later</u>
By jingo! What a day! Didlington Hall is set in an estate of 7,000 acres with its own otter-hunting lake, a falconry as big as a small castle, lots of workers' cottages and racehorse stables. They even have their own church.

But, most exciting of all, they have their very own museum! It is packed with all manner of things

from ancient times. I was allowed
to look at stone figures of gods,
kings, queens and cowherds that
were made in Egypt
5,000 years ago! And
I also saw the
preserved dead
bodies of ancient
Egyptian kings.
They're called mummies
and are salted like bacon, then
wrapped up in bandages so that
they'll last for ever! They are
the strangest and most exciting
things I have ever seen! Just
think, these people were walking
the earth even before the great
civilizations of the ancient
Greeks and Romans began! And now I
have actually touched one of them!
  I long to know what life was
like in those days. If only I
could travel back in time. It
would be such spiffing fun to
watch the embalmers at work!

1888 A few weeks later
Joy of joys, Lord and Lady Amherst
have said I may go and sketch all
their wonderful ancient artifacts
whenever I wish!

<u>1888 Several months later</u>
Another wonderful day, doodling
and daydreaming at Didlington.
This afternoon I sketched a
beautiful funeral boat marked with
the cartouche of Pharaoh Tuthmosis
III. As I worked, all
manner of brainy
and learned
scholars were
wandering around
the museum
chatting about this
and examining that.
One of the things that got them
really all-of-a-wobble were some
papyri pages of magic spells from
something called The Book of Dead.
Lawks a lummy! The atmosphere here
is so stimulating. The things I
hear set my imagination on fire!
Oh, how I wish I could visit that
faraway country of Egypt, with its
blue skies and valleys full of
ancient treasures!

<u>Summer 1891</u>
I have just turned 17 and the
Amhersts have appointed me as
official artist to their collection
of antiquities. I am cock-a-hoop!

107

Autumn 1891
Blinking Ada! Lady Amherst has
shown my drawings to Mr Percy
Newberry, the famous
archaeologist. He
wants me to come on
one of his digs and
draw what he finds.
Yes, I am going to
EGYPT! It's a dream
come true!

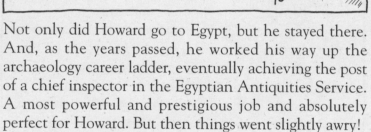

Not only did Howard go to Egypt, but he stayed there.
And, as the years passed, he worked his way up the
archaeology career ladder, eventually achieving the post
of a chief inspector in the Egyptian Antiquities Service.
A most powerful and prestigious job and absolutely
perfect for Howard. But then things went slightly awry!

8 January 1905
Bit of trouble today! Some 15
drunken Frenchmen arrived at the
diggings and tried to force their
way into the huts. Well, our cook
boy set about them with his frying
pan so off they went to the
official house where they began
fighting with our Egyptian guards.
It was at this point that I was
fetched to sort things out. Of
course, the drunken French wished me
to tell off my security chappies

for daring to lay their hands on
white men. By jingo! I did nothing
of the kind. I simply allowed them
to defend themselves against the
louts. The French consul here has
now asked me to apologize. I have
refused to do so. I did the
right thing!

Some time later:
I am bereft! I
have been
dismissed from the
Antiquities Service. All because the
French government made a formal
complaint against me and demanded
that I be sacked! Woe is me!

BIFF

But Howard needn't have worried. Despite losing his job
he continued to earn a living by acting as middleman and
setting up deals between Egyptians who wished to sell
tomb treasures to rich Europeans and Americans. It was
through his new business that he met Lord Carnarvon,
the wealthy English aristocrat who would finance his
search for Tutankhamun and his tombful of treasure.

## LOOKING FOR A PHARAOH IN A ROCKSTACK

Here's a question. How did Howard know where to look for Tut's tomb? Or that it even existed? Was it...

**a)** An incredibly ancient Egyptian woman, a direct descendant of Tut told him the family secret of the tomb's whereabouts in exchange for some spoons and a new ironing board.

**b)** He just happened to pass it when he heard knocking and cries of 'Get me out of here!'

**c)** It came to him in a dream.

It was none of these! It was by good old-fashioned detective work. But before we get to the nail-biting thrill-a-minute tale of Howard's astonishing 'really big adventure', you need to know a bit about those light-fingered reprobates known as...

## The tomb robbers!

Tomb robbing in ancient Egypt was big business, which is not that surprising when the Egyptians said things like, 'We'll just stick the equivalent of 10,000 rollover national lottery wins in this hole in the ground and walk away. Then again, on second thoughts, we'd better employ a couple of guards to watch over it. We've not checked their criminal records but they seem nice enough chaps. Right, let's get back to the digging and decorating.'

Before you could say, 'Strip Ramses naked!' the tomb robbers would be at it, sometimes actually pinching the contents before the plaster had dried on the sealed doorway. In some cases, they actually nicked the stuff as it was being taken into the tomb.

The tomb robbers weren't in least bit bothered about respecting the dead, offending the gods or spoiling their own chances of a cosy afterlife in Paradise. They'd be in like a shot, lifting the goodies and ripping the mummies to shreds like hounds on a fox, so that they could get at all the tasty king's bling that had been stashed inside the layers of bandages.

And then those tomb robbers would start on the body itself, pulling off the arms and legs, then tearing open the chest cavity so that they could get at the jewelled scarab that had been inserted in place of the Pharaoh's heart.

As a result, not a single Pharaoh had ever been found in their tomb undisturbed, just as the priests and mourners had left him. And, by the time the likes of Howard and Lord Carnarvon began poking around the Valley of the Kings, all the biggest and best-known tombs were well beyond their 'pillage-by' date! In fact, most of them were now being nothing more than empty chambers or, even worse, holes filled with rubble after the floods that periodically roared into the valley had caused their ceilings to collapse. Nevertheless, simply because of the astonishing amount of tombs that were sited there, the Valley of the Kings was still an archaeologist's paradise, even though what was left was only a tiny, tiny fraction of what had been put there in the first place.

## Theodore 'Disappointing' Davis

Since the beginning of the 20th century, a wealthy American lawyer called Theodore Davis had owned the exclusive rights to poke around in the Valley of the Kings. He and his archaeologist pals had been busily excavating here, there and everywhere. And, because the Valley of the Kings was still an enormous archaeologists' lucky-dip (despite centuries of tomb robbing), they came up with some remarkable finds. However, they never did hit that 'untouched-Pharaoh's-last-resting-place' jackpot, which all archaeologists dream of! So Theo finally chucked in his shovel, tired of his 'disappointing' results. But what he *didn't* realize is that he had already unearthed some INCREDIBLY IMPORTANT CLUES! In fact, at one point, he'd actually held in his hands the crucial evidence that would lead to the most important, exciting and mind-boggling archaeological discovery the world has ever seen! As we shall now see...

## Theo's 'load of rubbish'

In 1906, Theodore moved a large rock and underneath he found a beautiful little cup made from light blue glazed pottery. On it was a cartouche, which, when translated, said Nebkheprure – Tut's coronation name!

Next, during the 1907–08 excavating season, Theo found what appeared to be a hole filled with mud and rocks, all washed into it during a flood. However, when he and his junk-detectives began fossicking around in all the crud, they realized that they were in a small tomb!

So they fossicked a bit more and found a broken box. And inside the broken box were bits of broken gold foil. Bits of gold foil which, when pieced together, were not only found to have been stamped with Tut's name and that of his wife, but also showed the following scene:

Finally, not far from the mud-filled tomb, Theo found a rubbish-pit crammed with the trash of centuries. Being natural sticky-beaks, he and his pals got ferreting. Amongst all the rubbish they discovered some pottery jars filled with animal bones, two small brooms, some linen, a bag with some salt in it, some broken clay utensils, a broken jar wrapped in a cloth, some floral wreathes and a little yellow funeral mask. But was Theo excited about any of this? Was he archaeology! What he actually said was that these finds were, 'Disappointing and of no significance.' And then he gave them away. Doh!

## Valley of the Kings – It's not worth a candle!

In 1914, when Theo finally decided to give up his Valley of the Kings excavation 'concession', as it was known, Lord Carnarvon and Howard were in like a shot, with his richness buying up the exclusive rights to digging the Valley of the Kings, even though the bloke organizing the deal – the director of Ancient Egyptian Antiquities himself – said that the rights were 'not worth a candle'! How wrong he would turn out to be!

But what became of the rubbish that Theo had given away? Well, 15 years later, Herbert Winlock, the American colleague he'd given it to, finally got round to taking a closer look at it. And, being a very, very, very clever bloke, he discovered something quite remarkable. As soon as he'd finished his investigations he wrote to Howard Carter to tell him what he'd found out.

115

Dear Howard,

    I have just been taking an in-depth and extensive look-see at some 'rubbish', i.e. broken jars and whatnot, which Theodore Davis gave the New York Metropolitan Museum back in 1909. And I think what I have discovered will be of very great interest to you. Namely, this!

    I have pieced together some broken bits of pottery that I think were originally jars and found something incredible. In fact, I would sit down to read this next bit, if I were you! Not only do they bear the seal of KING TUTANKHAMUN, but also that of the Royal Necropolis!

    I think that this proves without a shadow of a doubt that, as you've believed all along, he IS buried somewhere in the Valley of the Kings! Now, get a load of this, buddy! 'The rubbish', which Theo so kindly gave away, is the remains of King Tut's ritual after-funeral banquet! In other words, the dishes and leftovers that are ritually buried after the feast. And from the meticulous scientific testing of this vital evidence, I now have deduced the following...

There were eight people present at the banquet. They wore floral and leaf wreaths and linen headbands. One of the headbands was inscribed with the last known date of Tutankhamun. During the banquet, the eight mourners tucked into five ducks, two plovers and a haunch of mutton, all washed down with beer and wine. Then, having finished the feast, they carefully swept up with the little brushes, which were also in the 'rubbish'. And, finally, they stuffed the leftover grub into the jars, gathered up the cups and dishes, then tipped the whole lot in a 'burial pit' specially dug for this purpose,

117

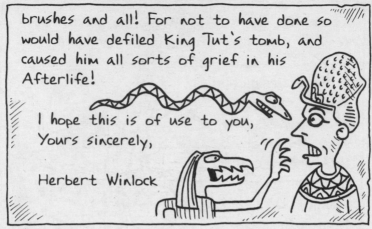

brushes and all! For not to have done so would have defiled King Tut's tomb, and caused him all sorts of grief in his Afterlife!

I hope this is of use to you, Yours sincerely,

Herbert Winlock

Well, can you imagine what effect reading these words had on Howard? And the news couldn't have come at a better time, because Lord Carnarvon was about to pull the plug on Howard's find-King-Tut's-lost-tomb excavating project. He'd had enough of pouring his fortune into it and seeing nothing in return.

YES! THERE'S HOPE YET!

BUT WILL LORD C. STUMP UP THE READIES?

## ONE STEP AT A TIME

<u>Howard Carter's secret lost diaries</u>
<u>October 1922</u>
During the last 15 years I have
shifted thousands of tons of sand
and rock in the Valley of the
Kings. Well, not me personally,
but the hundreds of Egyptian
labourers that Lord Carnarvon pays
for. Lord C has spent £50,000* and
we have almost nothing to show for
it. No wonder he is getting
impatient. This is my very last
chance to find that bally
undiscovered Pharaoh's tomb! The
sands of time are running out! I
just hope Herbert's findings turn
out to be true.

*Over £2.5 million in today's money.

<u>A few days later:</u>
Have arrived at my little house at
Qrna near the Valley of the Kings.
And I have got a gorgeous little
friend to keep me company. It's a
lovely golden canary in a cage,
which sings all day long (the
canary, not the cage). The local
Egyptian people, who have no
songbirds in their countryside,
are all very excited by it! They
say it will bring us good fortune.

<u>Wednesday, 1 November 1922</u>
My hundred or so labourers started
digging in the Valley of the
Kings, quite near the tomb of
Ramses VI, today. Found some
ancient stone workmen's houses.
They were covered in 3 metres of
rubble, but we soon had them
partly uncovered and found that
they were
connected
to more
huts. They
were also
covered in
rubble.

<u>Saturday, 4 November, 10 am</u>
When I arrived at the site this morning my Egyptian foreman told me that his chappies have moved more rubble and found a … step! Ooh! Ooh! By Jove! I am soooo excited!

<u>Sunday, 5 November, Sunset</u>
We are down to the twelfth step now! And what is this I see before me? My giddy aunt! It's only the blinking top of a plastered and sealed doorway. What's more, the seals are untouched! By Jingo! It could be a tomb entrance!

## Blooming builders! Tut! Tut!

Ramses VI had died in 1133 BC, about 200 years after Tutankhamun. The workmen building his tomb had carelessly built their houses over the entrance to Tut's tomb.

121

In a way though, this was a brilliant stroke of good fortune for Howard. If those houses hadn't been there, tomb robbers would have doubtlessly found the tomb entrance and stolen all the treasures!

COME ON ZEMNARIHAH! WHEN ARE YOU GOING TO STOP READING THAT NEWSPAPER AND DIG US A BASEMENT?

Howard Carter's secret lost diaries
Even later: I know from those seals that this must be the tomb of someone important! But I have no idea who. I have now made a little hole in the beam at the top of the door and am shining my electrical torch in. By golly! There is a passage on the other side, completely filled with stones and rubble up to its ceiling. I think I am on to something! Oh, after all these years of toil and trouble it looks like I've found it! A magnificent discovery: an untouched tomb.

Howard didn't know it at the time but if he had dug down a few more inches he would have found the impression of the seal of Tutankhamun. But he didn't! What he did do was seal up the hole and ride his donkey home, his heart thumping with excitement. The next morning he sent this telegram to Lord Carnarvon:

```
Dear Lord Carnarvon
At last have made wonderful
discovery in Valley: a magnificent
tomb with seals intact.
Re-covered same for your arrival.
Congratulations
```

Then he went back to the tomb, now named the Tomb of the Bird by his workmen, after his 'lucky' pet canary. He ordered them to pile the rubble back on top of the steps. He didn't want anyone else stumbling upon his amazing find. In fact, it was such an amazing find that he later said that once the rubble was back in place, he found it hard to believe...

*...that the whole episode had not been a dream!*

I WISH HE'D MAKE HIS MIND UP!

Howard Carter's secret lost diaries
Friday, 24 November 1922
I slept the night in the Valley
of the Kings. I was far too
excited to go home because this
weekend, Lord Carnarvon and I are
finally going to open the doors to
the tomb.


Saturday, 25 November
We opened the first doorway - and
we were in! In that moment I was
aware that three, maybe even four,
thousand years had passed since
human feet last trod the floor on
which we
now stood!
But all
around us
were signs
of life
that felt
like they
had taken
place
just
yesterday: a
flower dropped on the floor, a
blackened lamp, a finger mark on a
wall painting. It was all quite,
quite miraculous!

We immediately began clearing the passage. In amongst the rubble we found broken pots, jar seals, water skins, coloured pottery vases and fragments of small objects. This could only mean one thing. Tomb robbers had been here. My heart was in my mouth. Had they penetrated as far as the burial chamber? Only the coming days and weeks would tell.

Sunday, 26 November
We cleared another 9 metres of rubble during the morning. Then, at 2 pm. it was finally time to open the second doorway!

This was it! The moment I had awaited so long. I made a little hole in the top left-hand corner of the door and, poking in my iron testing rod, I discovered empty space on the other side! Next, using a candle for light, I looked in. Hot air rushing out of the tomb made my candle flicker, but soon my eyes got used to the dimness of the interior. My heart leapt and tears came to my eyes! I was struck dumb with amazement.

Before me, shrouded in an eerie swirling mist, stood strange

125

animals, beautiful statues and gold! Everywhere, there was the glint of gold!

Behind me Lord Carnarvon, jumping up and down with excitement, said, 'Can you see anything? Can you see anything?'

'Yes,' I replied. 'Wonderful things!'

I now made the hole big enough for us both to look in. And, by the light of a candle and our electrical torch, we beheld the most astonishing sights we had ever witnessed. I can hardly describe the sensations and astonishment that gripped me in that, the most exciting moment of my entire life!

Before us stood terrible beasts, their grotesque heads throwing terrifying, flickering shadows on the wall behind them; on their right, looming out of the darkness, were two strange ebony-black, king-like effigies, each one with the protective sacred cobra painted on its forehead; next to them were gilded couches in strange forms, decorated with the heads of lions and infernal beasts; exquisitely painted caskets; flowers; vases; a strange

black shrine with a gilded monster
snake appearing from it; a golden
throne; a heap of chariot parts
glinting with gold, and much, much
more than I have time to describe
now. And beyond all this treasure
lay another sealed doorway. A
sealed doorway behind which, I now
knew for certain, lay the grave of
Pharaoh Tutankhamun!

127

What a day that must have been for Howard! A day in which he probably experienced more thrills than most people enjoy in a lifetime. And he still had the actual burial chamber to enter. Which of course would be bound to contain Tut's mummy!

But the drama of 26 November 1922 was not yet finished! Later that night, having fastened a wooden security grill over the first doorway, Howard returned to his house at Qrna. However, as he entered the house, he came upon a tragic scene. His servant rushed towards him clutching a handful of yellow feathers, his face wracked with horror.

'Your canary, Mr Carter!' he gasped. 'Is no more! A huge cobra came into the house, caught it in its jaws and swallowed it one gulp!' Then he looked puzzled and said, 'It most unusual to see a cobra in winter. And they are now such rare creatures in Egypt, anyway.' Then he went pale and said, 'Mr Carter, I am sure you know that the cobra is the royal snake which protects the tombs of our Pharaohs from all intruders. I fear you have incurred the wrath of the gods, Mr Carter. You must abandon your excavations immediately!'

And so began the tale of the Curse of Tutankhamun…

# THE TERRIBLE CURSE OF TUTANKHAMUN

YOU BE THE JUDGE! (But only if you're brave enough)
The mysterious death of Howard's canary was the first of
a whole series of 'incidents'. During the days and months
which followed his entrance into Tut's tomb, all sorts of
'events' occurred, many of which can be viewed as very,
very spooky indeed!

*Having been made aware of the somewhat disturbing facts
surrounding Howard's 'lucky' bird, consider the following:*
**1)** When Howard and Lord Carnarvon entered the tomb,
they passed beneath this curse engraved in the limestone:
'Death Shall Come on Swift Wings To Him Who
Disturbs the Peace of the King'.
**2)** Just a few months later, in the early hours of 5 April
1923, Lord Carnavon died in Cairo, the capital of Egypt.
**3)** Lord Carnarvon died at 2 o'clock in the morning.
Back in England, Susie, his dog, threw back her head,
howled mournfully at the moon, and also dropped dead
… at 2 o'clock in the morning!
**4)** Just as Lord Carnarvon passed away, all the lights in
Cairo went out.

**5)** Five months later, his younger brother died suddenly.
**6)** Howard's personal secretary, Richard Bethell, a relative of Lord Carnarvon, died of a heart attack.
**7)** Richard's father, Lord Westbury, killed himself by jumping from his seventh-storey flat.
**8)** The much-respected author and creator of Sherlock Holmes, Sir Arthur Conan Doyle, announced that Carnarvon's death was a result of a curse. By now millions of people had become convinced that anyone connected with the opening of Tut's tomb was doomed.
**9)** In the years that followed, the newspapers were full of stories about the Curse of Tutankhamun. In 1935, journalists keeping track of these sinister occurrences said that the deaths of no less than 21 people were linked to the opening of King Tut's tomb. Ooer!

I WANT MY MUMMY!

CURSE OF TUTANKHAMUN STRIKES AGAIN!

*Now consider the following:*
**1)** The inscription that Howard and Lord Carnarvon are said to have passed beneath didn't exist. However, one hieroglyphic inscription, on the shrine to Anubis, the jackal god, did say: 'It is I who hinder the sand from choking the secret chamber. I am for the protection of the deceased.'

But then, a very mischievous journalist decided that things needed 'spicing up' a bit. So he reported it as going on to say 'I will kill all those who cross this threshold into the sacred precincts of the royal king who lives forever.' Which is how his newspaper reported it, thus convincing millions of impressionable people that the curse was true.

2) Ever since being involved in a near-fatal car crash, Lord Carnarvon had been in very poor health. Sometime before he died from pneumonia and blood poisoning he had been bitten by an insect and the wound had become infected. All sorts of nasty lurgies and fevers were floating around in 1920s Egypt, and lots of the protective jabs and medicines now available to protect tourists from the lurgies weren't available in those days.

3) Lord Carnarvon's dog didn't drop dead at exactly the same time as his master, because Egypt and Britain are in different time zones.

4) After losing lots of his nearest and dearest relatives in the First World War, Sir Arthur Conan Doyle became very superstitious and employed spiritualist mediums to help him contact his loved ones. In fact, during this period in British history, the entire nation was gripped by all sorts of strange beliefs about souls and the afterlife, because so many bereaved people were desperate to get in touch with their loved ones who had died in that terrible conflict. So their feverish and overwrought imaginations would be entirely open and susceptible to a story like the Curse of the Mummy's Tomb.

5) An art museum director in New York City decided to approach the mystery in a more scientific and analytical manner and came up with the following statistics.

• 22 people present when the tomb was opened in 1922. Only six had died by 1934.

• 22 people were present at the opening of the sarcophagus in 1924. Only two of them died in the following ten years.

• 10 people were there when the mummy was unwrapped in 1925. They all survived until at least 1934.

6) Howard Carter always said the story of the curse was a load of 'tommy-rot' (or tomby-rot?). He lived until he was 64 and died of natural causes.

7) An Egyptian doctor looked at the health records of museum workers and noticed that many of them had been exposed to a fungus that caused them to suffer from fever, fatigue and rashes. He said that the fungus may have survived in the tombs for thousands of years and also had been picked up by archaeologists when they entered. This could also happen to visitors to the tomb, or even people who touched objects from the tombs.

8) In 1999 a German microbiologist analyzed 40 mummies and found potentially dangerous mould spores on all of them! Mould spores can survive thousands of years, even in a dark, dry tomb. Some of them can be toxic. When tombs were first opened these spores could have been blown up into the air. If spores enter the body through the nose, mouth or eyes they can lead to organ failure or even death, particularly in people who are in poor health! For example, Lord Carnarvon.

WE'RE BACK!

JUST WHEN YOU THOUGHT IT WAS SAFE!

9) Archaeologists now wear protective masks and gloves when unwrapping a mummy. Something that Howard and Lord Carnarvon definitely didn't do!

# AH, MR CARTER, WE MEET AT LAST!

<u>Howard Carter's secret lost diaries</u>
<u>Monday, 27 November 1922</u>
Absolutely fagged-out.
Nevertheless, we arrived at the
excavations really early so that
we could rig up the electrical
lighting and get exploring the
chamber we'd glimpsed through the
hole. But can you blame us? Ooh,
ooh! It is all so exciting! By
noon the lights were all ready.
Lord C and I crept into that
catacomb a-tingle with
apprehension.
  At that astonishing moment we
knew we were on to something BIG!
Everywhere we looked there were
masses and masses of treasures,
all jumbled and higgledy-piggledy.

So much that it was impossible to take it all in!

'Thieves have been in here, Carter, old bean!' said Lord C, stroking his greying moustache thoughtfully.

'I fear so, m'lud,' I replied as I gazed on fragments of pots and vases that had been broken by ancient intruders during their frantic search for gold and jewellery.

Then a thought struck me! Maybe this wasn't a burial site we'd happened upon after all, but simply a stash of royal treasure! But then, as we looked beneath one of the fantastic carved couches we spotted a gap in the rock wall.

Yes, yet another sealed doorway, partly broken open by the long-dead tomb raiders.

'Follow me, m'lud!' I whispered. Lord C and I wriggled under the strange, gilded couch and peered into the opening. And by golly! It was another chamber! And this one was filled to overflowing with an absolute confusion of beds, chairs, boxes, vases, statues and peculiar loaf-shaped cases with everything overturned and ransacked for valuables.

'See!' I muttered. 'The seals imprinted in the plaster are just like those on the other doorways!'

'But still no mummy!' murmured Lord C.

But then I remembered the sealed doorway between those two guardian statues. And it hit me!

'By gad!' I cried. 'There can be only one reason for this great hoard of treasures being here! We have simply reached the foremost portion of a tomb. Behind that closed doorway must be the tomb-chamber itself!'

'And, no doubt, the mummy of Tutankhamun!' Gasped Lord C. 'By golly, Carter! I think you're right.'

All over the closed doorway we found the insignia of King Tutankhamun, made by his cartouche seal being pressed into the wet plaster as his tomb was walled up. A few more bashes with our picks and we were in! And there before us lay the stone sarcophagus that we knew would contain the mummy of Tutankhamun.

What sight it all was! And one we'd never dreamed we'd see. We were flabbersmacked, gobghasted and almost tearful. I felt like a child who has stumbled upon all his Christmas presents for the next ten years. I was desperate to begin opening chests and rummaging

around this Aladdin's cave of
wonders. Not to mention opening
that great sarcophagus. But I knew
I couldn't, for our examination of
the tomb and its contents would
have to be slow and painstaking.
And the excavating season was
drawing to its close, so it would
be months before we could begin
our investigations proper.

Wednesday, 29 November
Official opening of the tomb today
and specially invited guests came
for lunch outdoors in the Valley
of the Kings, i.e. sandwiches …
followed by 'dessert!' (ha ha!
just my little joke, old thing!).
All manner of VIPs present.

So that was that! Howard had finally found the long-lost tomb of Tutankhamun. But it would be many months before he could begin his work again. And, even more frustratingly, it would be another *three* years before Howard came face to face with Tut himself!

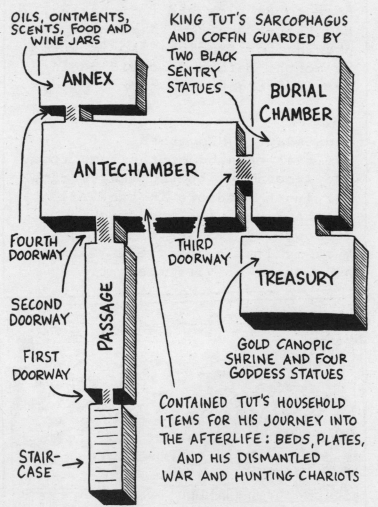

OILS, OINTMENTS, SCENTS, FOOD AND WINE JARS

ANNEX

KING TUT'S SARCOPHAGUS AND COFFIN GUARDED BY TWO BLACK SENTRY STATUES

BURIAL CHAMBER

ANTECHAMBER

FOURTH DOORWAY

THIRD DOORWAY

TREASURY

SECOND DOORWAY

PASSAGE

FIRST DOORWAY

GOLD CANOPIC SHRINE AND FOUR GODDESS STATUES

CONTAINED TUT'S HOUSEHOLD ITEMS FOR HIS JOURNEY INTO THE AFTERLIFE: BEDS, PLATES, AND HIS DISMANTLED WAR AND HUNTING CHARIOTS

STAIR-CASE

<u>Howard Carter's secret lost diaries</u>

<u>12 October 1925</u>
Opened the tomb, turned on our
2,000-candle-power electrical
lamps, removed the cover we had
put over the sarcophagus and
looked in amazement at that great
gold coffin. Went dizzy all over
with excitement. By Jove, it's
stunning, old bean!

<u>21 October</u>

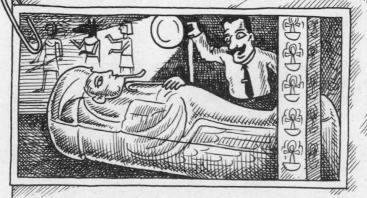

A thrill a minute! After opening
the outer coffin we found another
nestling inside that. Then, by
Jove, another inside that! Each
one has a likeness of King Tut's
face on it, the second being more
astoundingly and exquisitely
decorated than the first! In it,

we found a flower wreath and
floral garlands, untouched for
3,000 years!

<u>24 October</u>
We have had a devil of a time
lifting the amazingly heavy
coffins out of the sarcophagus for
fear we'll cause them damage. And
damage is caused. Every so often
we hear a sickening 'crack!'
followed by a heartrending
'clink!' as yet another priceless
surface ornament falls to the
floor!

<u>25 October</u>
Today we raised the two innermost
coffins and took them to the
antechamber. It took eight strong
men to lift them!

<u>28 October</u>
Using long screwdrivers that we'd
bent into curved levers we began
to waggle loose the metal pins
holding down the coffin lid. It
took us hours! But finally, the
pins were out. And the lid was
raised - and there he was! Pharaoh
Tutankhamun himself, looking all
peaceful and tranquil! Covering

his head was the most beautiful mask I have ever seen! It was brilliantly crafted from solid gold inlaid with stripes of blue glass, all topped by a solid gold cobra and vulture.

Attached to the mask's throat were three massive necklaces, a heart-scarab between the hands, crossed over the breast, hold the flail and the crook. Below this mask, which reaches as far as the hands, are the mummy bandages going all the way to his feet.

### 31 October

I have tried to remove the mummy and mask from the innermost coffin, but have failed. The years have taken their toll on all those perfumed oils and creams that were poured over King Tutankhmun. They turned black like

tar and firmly glued him to the
bottom of his coffin. So, we are
going to take him outside into the
hot sun in the hope that the gunge
will melt!

1 November
It took ten men to carry
Tutankhamun up out of his tomb.
I then left him under the blazing
Egyptian sun.

A few hours later
No luck, mummy still stuck fast!
Oh well, we'll just have to
unwrap him in his coffin.

11 November
Today has been a great day in the
history of archaeology! A day of
days that I have dreamed of for
years. For today, as he lay in
his coffin, stuck fast by that
pesky 'glue', we began to unwrap
the mummy of Tutankhamun!
   First we poured paraffin wax
over the fragile mummy bandages so
that they wouldn't disintegrate
when we removed them. As soon as
the wax was cool, my colleague,
Dr Derry, made a long cut down
the centre of the outer wrappings.

Then we began to remove large
pieces of the linen wrapping.
And, hardly had we begun, when we
discovered two fabulous gold
amulets hidden beneath them!

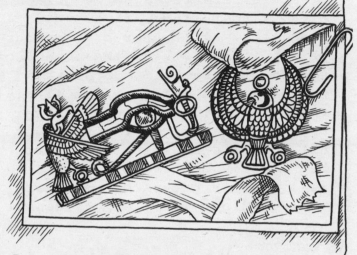

But that was only the beginning.
From this moment on, with each
piece of bandage we removed, we
found yet another astonishing
treasure! Soon we were surrounded
by a cornucopia of treasure! Golden
amulets, gold serpents, a golden
dagger with a crystal knob, bands
of decorated sheet gold, bracelets,
beadwork, a large black scarab
beetle laid on his belly-button - to
name but a few. There were hundreds
of priceless objects concealed
within the mummy's outer shell!

## 13 November

A new day dawns! But still we continue to peel back the king's packaging. And, as we do, yet more treasures are revealed: a golden bird, finger rings, five bracelets. All manner of wondrous objects! And I think the finest of modern craftsmen and goldsmiths would be hard put to match them! The thing is, we are only as far as his forearms! We've still got his top bits and his head to do, but already we have discovered no less than 52 groups of personal and religious jewellery hidden all over him!

## 14 November

We have now stripped the lower part of King Tut's body and his legs. Having examined them, Dr Derry and Dr Saleh Bey have found the soft tissues of his body to be in a very brittle and carbonized condition.

HE'S DONE FOR

## 15 November
We've been at it five days now.
Sixteen layers of bandages
removed. And still we are finding
treasures aplenty!

## 16 November
Now for the head - which we've
left until last as it's
completely covered by that
magnificent golden mask. That
magnificent golden mask which is
stuck to the coffin. We've used hot
knives to cut the mask from the
coffin. And now, after quite a
struggle we have got King Tut's
bandaged head free of the mask!

## Even later
Now we are unwrapping the head.
And still finding treasure!

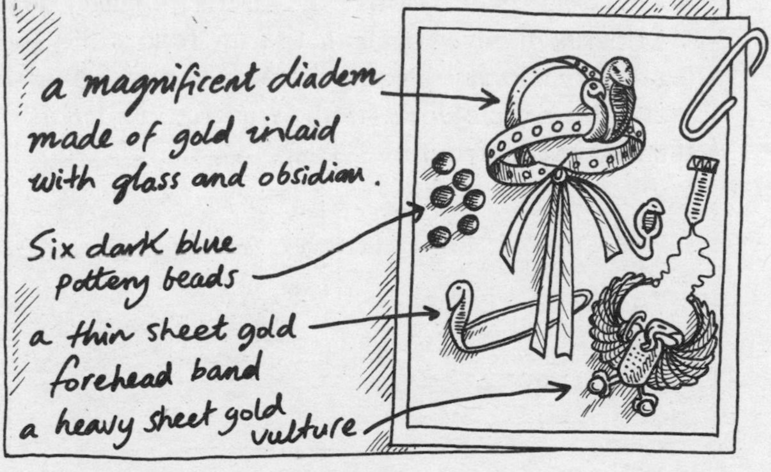

a magnificent diadem
made of gold inlaid
with glass and obsidian.

Six dark blue
pottery beads

a thin sheet gold
forehead band

a heavy sheet gold
vulture

A few more bandages to unravel and
… yes! At last I am face to face
with King Tutankhamun! And what a
very refined and cultured sort of
person he is! The spitting image
of his father too!

WHAT KEPT YOU?

And there we'll leave Howard fossicking away happily. Because it's now time to reveal the amazing stuff that other, later, generations of archaeologists and Egyptologists discovered about the mysterious life and times of Tutankhamun. Not to mention finally getting to grips with the age-old question: 'Was Tut murdered?' – and if he was, 'Who dunnit?'

## THE BODY OF EVIDENCE

It took Howard another astonishing seven years to clear Tut's tomb completely. Then again, he did have several thousand different treasures to sort through.

WE'D HAVE DONE IT IN A WEEKEND AT HALF THE PRICE!

RON'S HOUSE CLEARANCE COMPANY

### Tutankhamun and his tombful of 'trousers'

(Or, does my tum look big in this?)

Amongst the mind-boggling items Howard removed during that time was a treasure trove of ancient fashion. Yes, masses and masses of clothes, ranging from Tut's embroidered, gold-encrusted tunics, triangular fabric loincloths (or 'Calvin Kleins' as we call them nowadays), leopard-skins and posh frocks, to his baby clothes and no less than 47 pairs of his royal socks. Yes! In preparing to send Tut off to live happily ever after, those ancient Egyptian spiritual travel agents thought of everything, even packing him loads of clean underwear!

CAN'T BE TOO CAREFUL. WHAT IF HE WERE TO GET RUN OVER BY A CHARIOT. WOULDN'T WANT HIM TURNING UP AT HOSPITAL IN DIRTY UNDIES, NOW WOULD WE?

Every single sock, pant, tunic, frock and vest, or its ancient-Egyptian equivalent, had been immaculately folded, then tidily placed in beautifully decorated storage chests.

But then, those low-life tomb robbers struck and in their frantic search for gold, they simply pulled the 450 different garments out of their containers and slung them hither and thither.

I'VE FOUND TUTANKHAMUN'S FABLED GOLDEN BOOTY!

YOU ANCIENT EGYPTIAN IDIOT!

When the ancient Egyptian officials came in to tidy up, they were faced with a great tangled jumble of hundreds of undies and outies. So desperate were they to do a swift job that they stuffed the clothes back into the nearest box they could find, leaving poor Tut surrounded by a 12-year-old's bedroom worth of chaos.

Being a perceptive and imaginative man, Howard took one look at the king's 3,000-year-old threads and immediately realized how important they were and what they might tell us about Tut and his life and times if they were studied carefully. However, no one bothered to follow his advice and Tut's togs were left to moulder and disintegrate for the next 70 years. Some items ended up looking like nothing more than a black crumbly mass of rotten fabric.

But then, in the 1990s, a textile historian decided to take a shufty at the clothes and, helped by some pals, carried on doing so for the next eight years! During that time she discovered all sorts of interesting data about the dapper divine one. For instance, his socks were always made so that there was gap between Tut's tootsies, in order to make a comfortable fit for the thongs of his royal flip-flops (and here's you thinking it's only weird, 55-year-old English blokes who wear socks with their sandals).

But they also came up against problems when they found that modern textile-making machines couldn't create the very fine, top-quality thread that was necessary for the thin silk-like material of many of his garments. So specialists in the art of ancient textile production had to make them.

Using high-tech kit, the textiles team were also able to work out what colour the clothes were originally so that they could have a bash at recreating the vivid and dazzling

149

hues of Tut's actual togs using ancient colour recipes such as red plant dye mixed with rancid olive oil and sheep muck.

Then, after dressing up in the various clothes and wandering around in them, the team not only discovered how comfortable they were, but also found out that some things weren't what they thought they were. For example what they thought were two head-dresses were actually meant to be worn on the arms to form the wings of the falcon, the emblem of the Egyptian king.

Another thing they discovered was how the costumes made the wearer look and feel powerful and special, which, of course, is exactly what they were intended to do.

They were also decorated with bands of hieroglyphs, which when translated were found to say things like

As 'son of the sun god', little Tut would have quite literally dazzled his subjects in his glittering robes, their lavish gold and beaded decoration making a delicate tinkling sound whenever he moved.

Another conclusion the researchers came to was that Tut's clothes indicated that he suffered from a mysterious disease that left him with big fat hips. Measuring them (the clothes, not his hips) they worked out that his vital statistics were: chest 80 cm, waist 75 cm, hips 110 cm. In other words he was pear-shaped! Which, if the pictures of

his dad, Akhenaten, are accurate, would indicate that Tut was the same shape as him. And that could mean…
**a)** Tut suffered from an inherited affliction (pear-shaped-Pharaoh syndrome?).
**b)** They were addicted to giant burgers.
**c)** They were a really 'hip' bunch of rulers.

**The strange case of King Tutankhamun's missing willy**
Those mummifiers certainly knew their stuff(ing). When Howard and his crew first found Tut's body (apart from being in desperate need of some top-of-the-range moisturiser and anti-wrinkle cream) it was in remarkably good condition! And that's after lying in that hot and dusty tomb for an incredible 3,300 years!

However, it wasn't long before Howard and his assistants got busy 'deconstructing' poor old Tut. First, they cut him into pieces, so that they could get at his jewellery, which that incredibly sticky embalming resin had now super-glued to his skin. Next they cut off his head.

And finally, they used hot knives to slice away his fabulous golden death mask, which had also become firmly stuck, this time to the long-suffering king's face.

In October 1926, having finally finished all his poking and prying, Howard rewrapped Tut, laid him in his sand tray and put him back in his outermost coffin and stone sarcophagus. After which, a thick glass lid was placed on top of the whole lot so that the coffin was protected from prying fingers (and Tut could gawp at the tourists while they gawped at him). And there he lay, undisturbed in his tomb, for another 42 years.

But then, in 1968, a new dynasty of scientists and historians decided to have a yet another poke around Tut's anatomy and to give him an X-ray. When they did, they got a terrible shock. They discovered that a really important bit of the king's anatomy had disappeared!

*OH NO!* *SOMEONE'S PINCHED THE PHARAOH'S WILLY!*

The paranoid paleologists became convinced Tut's tinkler had been swiped by a souvenir hunter. In the years that followed all sorts of bods turned up, claiming to have found the king's little pal. But all of these turned out to be red herrings.

Then, in 2005, yet another bunch of Egyptolologists took an even closer look at Tut. And this time they used a high-tech hospital CT scanner. And the results were astonishing!

*HURRAH! IT'S BACK!* *THE KING'S TINKLER HAS RETURNED!*

But how? Had it grown back again? Or did the willy thief have a crisis of conscience and sneak it back in? No, of course not! The King's tinkler hadn't even been lost in the first place. It had simply 'dropped off'! It had been lying in the sand all the time. Those short-sighted 1960s scientists had failed to spot it!

# Tutti frutti – it's all gone all sooty!

Ancient Egyptians were growing grapes and drinking wine long before Tutankhamun strutted his stuff in the sand dunes of the New Kingdom.

We know this because paintings showing grape harvests, wine-making and, would you believe, 'binge drinking', have been found on tomb walls dating back as far back 2600 BC (Before Champagne).

Like all upper-class Egyptians, Tut enjoyed the odd chalice or three of plonk. So, as you'd expect, when the time came for his big send-off to the big party in the Fields of Paradise, his aristocratic pals made sure that his subterranean 'drinks cabinet' was really well stocked (there not being all that many decent wine bars in the Afterworld). When his tomb was opened in 1922, no fewer than 36 huge amphorae (clay wine jars) were discovered stashed away in there. However, when the archaeologists looked inside the amphorae, all they found was layer of sticky crud at the bottom of each jar. Why do you think that was?

**a)** During the 3,300 years it had lain in the tomb, the wine had evaporated.

**b)** Shifting dirty great rocks in the fierce Egyptian sun is extremely thirsty work. So, the moment Howard Carter and Lord Carnarvon discovered the booze, they yelled something like, 'Cripes I've got a thirst you could photograph!' and immediately drank the lot!

**c)** Most of the jars were empty when they were first put in the tomb.

The answer is **c)** Those ancient Egyptians were an incredibly thoughtful and attentive bunch. Just like modern wine-makers do, they actually took the trouble to put lots of product information on their packaging. Twenty-six of the amphorae found in Tut's tomb were marked with the name of the wine, the year it was made, the year of Tut's reign when the wine was bottled, where the grapes were grown and even the name of the vine grower (not to mention all the E numbers it contained and its best-before date). From the dates on the jars, Egyptologists have worked out that most of the wine would have evaporated before they were stashed in the tomb. Ancient Egyptian wine jars were made from unglazed clay, so the wine slowly evaporated through their porous walls.

Even more importantly, by reading the information on the wine jars, Howard and Lord Carter worked out that Tut had died young, probably during the ninth year of his reign. This was later confirmed when scientists did an analysis of his remains. But how *did* he die?

## Was Tut murdered?
*You* be the judge!

## The evidence *for* the case

Tutankhamun was only 19 when he died. All right, life expectancy in ancient Egypt was very short and less than half of all people reached their 25th birthday. But Tutankhamun was top banana in the richest and most powerful civilization on Earth! He would have eaten the best food, enjoyed the best hygiene, been 'minded' by the hardest heavies, and treated by the best doctors. And a high-tech examination carried out on his remains found he'd had general good health. So, he should have lived until he was, ooh … at least the ripe old age of 40! If you're young and healthy you don't just suddenly pop your sandals for no reason. Unless, that is, you have an accident. Or are murdered!

## The physical evidence

• Tut had a partly healed scar on his left jaw, possibly the result of a violent assault. But, if it was partly healed, it meant he had survived for some time after receiving the blow.

• A fragment of bone was found inside Tut's skull. Could it be linked to the blow to his jaw?

• Tut's leg was broken. Possibly because he'd been involved in an accident. Or had he been attacked?

• Tut's breastbone and part of his ribcage were found to be missing. He would not have been born without them. So, were they removed by Howard? Or when he was mummified? If the embalmers did remove them, it would have been because they were so badly damaged that it would have been impossible to remove Tut's internal organs without doing so!

## The political evidence

Tut's closest advisers, Aye and Horemheb, had lots of reasons for wanting him dead. Not only did Aye immediately take over as Pharaoh after Tut's death, he also married his widow! And Horemheb was Tut's deputy and army general, who had helped make all his kingly decisions for him when he was knee high to a jackal.

But at 19, Tut would be old enough to do the job himself. Maybe Horemheb didn't want to lose his power either?

After Aye died, Horemheb became Pharaoh. Not only did he complete ancient Egypt's return to the religious traditions that had been in place before Tut's 'alternative' dad changed everything, but he moved his capital to Memphis and returned all the temples to their priests.

And, on a far more sinister note, he had Tut's name erased from monuments and buildings everywhere and his own put in its place.

Both of these men were rich and powerful. It was well within their means to have Tut 'clipped'!

So, what with Tut's potential enemies, his crushed chest, broken leg and jaw wound, it may well be that something very violent brought about his end! But what?

## The evidence *against* Tut having been murdered

In March 2005 a team of Egyptian scientists took Tut out of his coffin (yet again!) and subjected him to the high-tech medical examination known as a CT (computed tomography) scan. In other words, they shoved him in one of those big white tube thingies and took masses of incredibly detailed 3D X-ray snaps of all his internal bits and pieces. When they'd finished, one or two of the doctors present did say that there was a possibility that he may have died from gangrene, which set in after his thigh had been broken. However, every single one of them categorically stated that there was absolutely no evidence whatsoever that Tut had been murdered! (What do you mean, 'Aw, how disappointing!')

## CONCLUSION

From time to time we all discover something or other, don't we? Some of us find that much-loved pencil that slipped down the back of the settee. Others are overjoyed to find a missing pet or a long-lost sock.

AH! MY OLD PENCIL!

AND MY LONG-LOST HAMSTER!

But it takes a man of Howard Carter's intelligence and true grit to track down and unearth something as incredible as the 3,000-year-old treasure-filled tomb and jewel-encrusted corpse of an ancient Egyptian king! An ancient Egyptian king whose sophisticated subjects were reading and writing, carrying out scientific investigations, practising advanced medicine, doing complicated mathematical calculations and building beautiful cities while the prehistoric rest of us were still struggling to emerge from the blooming Stone Age!

As the news and pictures of Howard Carter's discovery of Tutankhamun and his tombful of treasure whizzed around the world in the 1920s, it left people astonished and open-mouthed with awe and wonder. And several decades later, it's still doing so. When the great Tutankhamun exhibition of 1972 was put on to celebrate the 50th anniversary of Howard's find, it was visited by around eight million people in the USA alone. And another two million in Great Britain! No doubt people will be gazing at it in awe and wonder for hundreds of years to come.